ON EARTH AS IT IS ON HEAVEN

On Earth as It is On Heaven

The Promise of America, Technology, and the New Earth

BOOK ONE

The Promise of America

by

W. Kent Smith

in association with

Staten House

Books by W. Kent Smith

*Lies My Professor Told Me About American Politics: Questions
Concerning the Original Vision of the Founding Fathers*

*Conquering Cynicism in a Modern Age: How The Bible in Nature
Provides an Antidote to Doubt and Despair*

*On Earth as It is On Heaven: The Promise of America, Technology,
and the New Earth, Book One: The Promise of America*

*The Book of Days: In Search of the 5,500-year Prophecy
Given to Adam About the Coming of Christ*

*The Book of Tales: Stories That Confirm the 5,500-year
Prophecy Given to Adam About the Coming of Christ*

*Fish Tales (From the Belly of the Whale): Fifty of the
Greatest Misconceptions Ever Blamed on The Bible,
Reel One, The Hook #50-34*

*Fish Tales (From the Belly of the Whale): Fifty of the
Greatest Misconceptions Ever Blamed on The Bible,
Reel Two, The Line #33-18*

*Fish Tales (From the Belly of the Whale): Fifty of the
Greatest Misconceptions Ever Blamed on The Bible,
Reel Three, The Sinker #17-1*

*Fish Tales (From the Belly of the Whale): Fifty of the
Greatest Misconceptions Ever Blamed on The Bible, The
Complete Edition, Hook, Line, and Sinker #50-1*

*Tales of Forever: The Unfolding Drama of God's Hidden
Hand in History, Book One: The Analyses – Part One*

*Tales of Forever: The Unfolding Drama of God's Hidden
Hand in History, Book Two: The Tales – Part One*

*Tales of Forever: The Unfolding Drama of God's Hidden
Hand in History, Book Three: The Tales – Part Two*

*Tales of Forever: The Unfolding Drama of God's Hidden
Hand in History, Book Four: The Analyses – Part Two*

*Tales of Forever: The Unfolding Drama of God's Hidden
Hand in History, The Complete Edition*

For Doc,

The Constant Gardener

CONTENTS

CONTENTS

THE PROMISE OF AMERICA

Isn't God your Father and Creator? Didn't He make you and establish you? Remember the days of old; consider the years long past. Ask your fathers, and they'll tell you, your elders, and they'll inform you. When the Most High divided their inheritance to the nations, and when He separated the sons of Adam, He set the boundaries of the peoples according to the number of the Children of Israel. But the Lord's portion is His people, Jacob is His allotted inheritance.
(Deuteronomy 32:6-9)

OF GOD'S EXPANDING EMPIRE

ONE OF the most famous scenes in *The Bible* has a suppli-cant Jesus standing before the Roman governor Pontius Pilate. The steely-eyed governor asked his prisoner:

"Are you the king of the Jews?"

"Are you asking for yourself," Jesus calmly replied, "or are others asking that about Me?"

"What?" blurted Pilate. "Am I a Jew? Your own people and chief priests have brought you before me. What have you done?"

And then, Jesus said, "My Kingdom isn't of this world. If it were, then My servants would fight to prevent My arrest by the Jewish leaders. But now My Kingdom is from another place."[1]

And because of what Jesus said here about His Kingdom not being "of this world," most people assume that only Heaven is worthy of being pursued, and that the Earth should be forever viewed as an enemy of God's Kingdom. As a result, generation after generation of the faithful have spawned all kinds of philosophies that denigrate anything to do with the present world.

Many who hold this view naturally point to the fact that this is because ever since Adam and Eve's expulsion from Eden we live as fallen creatures in a fallen world. And as a believer in Scripture myself, I'd certainly agree that this is an accurate depiction of the human condition.

However, just as importantly, in spite of our fallen state as descendants of Adam and Eve, *The Bible* is just as clear on many other aspects that are just as worthy of our consideration. As for

---

1   John 18:33-36

the true nature of our world, despite its present predicament, Scripture declares:

> The Earth is the Lord's and all its fullness—the world and all who live in it.[2]

> The Lord loves righteousness and justice; the Earth is full of His loving devotion.[3]

> For everything God created is good, and nothing is to be rejected if it's received with thanksgiving.[4]

From passages like these, we see that Jesus' reference to His Kingdom not being "of this world" doesn't mean this world is entirely evil just because Adam's descendants continue as prisoners of death, Hell, and the grave until the consummation of the ages. For anyone who cares to notice, in contrasting His Kingdom with this world, Jesus didn't say the Earth itself was unworthy or ungodly; He simply stated that His Kingdom wasn't "of this world." The Greek word that Jesus used for "world" is *cosmos*, which doesn't speak of the Earth and all its fullness *per se* but, rather, of a world system, as in, a world philosophy or ideology.

So, in making this distinction between these two realms, Jesus wasn't warning us that because His Kingdom is so much better than our world we should treat the Earth as nothing more than the devil's domain. If that were true, then how are we to interpret what the gospel writer said about the origins of this *cosmos*? Said John:

> The true Light Who gives light to every man was coming into the world. He was in the world, and though the world was made through Him, the world didn't recognize Him.[5]

Because John used the same word—*cosmos*—when speaking of the world in this verse, we can conclude that if Jesus Himself

---

2   *Psalm 24:1*

3   *Ibid. 33:5*

4   *First Timothy 4:4*

5   *John 1:9-10*

made the world, it follows that the *cosmos* isn't by nature alien to the God Who created it. As such, we see that Christ's purpose, in contrasting His Kingdom with the present world, was never to demonize the Earth and its inhabitants just because we're enduring the aftermath of Adam's disobedience. It was simply a prelude to understanding that the present *cosmos* required a radical intrusion from an outside force, which could only occur by establishing the Kingdom of Heaven on Earth according to God's unfolding plan.

Further evidence of the compatibility of God's Kingdom and this Earth can be seen when we look to the famous prayer of Jesus, where He teaches us to pray for "God's will to be done on Earth as it is in Heaven."[6] If these two spheres of existence are as foreign to one another as tradition often has us believing, why would Jesus urge us to pray for them to merge in this way?

What's more, our traditional view of the incompatibility of Jesus' world and ours is based on the English phrase that states His Kingdom isn't "*of* this world." But actually, the Greek word used in this phrase is *ek*, sometimes transliterated as *ex*, as in, *deus ex machina*, which is to say, "god from the machine." As such, what Jesus said was: His Kingdom isn't "*from* this world."

Now, at first, this might seem like an insignificant shift in meaning, but in fact when we focus on the assumption that Jesus' Kingdom isn't "of" this world, it implies that there's an impenetrable barrier between Earth and this other place. But in contrast, saying that His Kingdom isn't "from" this world just lets us know it didn't originate on Earth but instead comes from somewhere else.

So, while one word—*of*—leads us to believe that we need to leave the Earth to go where Jesus is, the other word—*from*—lets us know that while that Kingdom definitely came from another place, it's now taking up residence in our *cosmos* as a new frontier of God's expanding Empire.

The following work concerns the story of that new frontier and of that expanding Empire, manifesting itself, one person, one day, one prayer at a time.

---

6   *Matthew 6:10*

AMERICA'S NEXT CROSSROAD

AMERICA, in the year 2023, stands at a crossroad. But certainly anyone who has studied the history of America knows this is by no means its first crossroad. In fact, one of the classic earmarks that makes America unique in the history of nations is the clear-cut nature of these crossroads: 1492, 1620, 1776, 1865, 1918, 1945, all mark critical turning points in American history, at which time the nation went decisively in one direction instead of another. Instead of succumbing to the rule of the tyrant, Americans chose the rule of law; instead of knuckling under the way of tyranny, we chose the way of liberty; and instead of extending the hand of intolerance, we chose the hand of tolerance.

By these three hallmarks, Americans would abide by a determined choice, even while those who opposed such values would continue to vie for the hearts of men, women, and children everywhere. So, while these three—law, liberty, and tolerance—had once been the mark of only individuals, but never of whole nations, America would be the first in the history of nations to be founded entirely on such ideals, those born of "the better angels of our nature," to which Abraham Lincoln once alluded.

More importantly, while each of these turning points marked events that impacted America itself, they would also impact the entire world around it. As such, 1492 marked not only the Spanish discovery of the American continent, but it also opened a doorway through which so many other Western nations would flow. 1620 marked not only the landing of the Pilgrims at Plymouth Rock, but it also opened a doorway through which many others seeking religious freedom would follow. 1776 marked not only the signing of the Declaration of Independence, which ratified American liberty, but it also opened a doorway through which many other nations would model their own futures.

1865 marked not only the end of the American Civil War, but it also opened a doorway through which we would enter the next phase of the Emancipation Proclamation, both here and abroad. And 1918 and 1945 marked not only the end of the First and Second World Wars, respectively, but they also opened doorways through which the hallmarks of American society—namely, law, liberty, and tolerance—would create an irresistible tidal wave unlike the world had ever experienced to date.

However, while men and women of character, both in America and around the world, embrace law, liberty, and tolerance, we know all too well that this never marked the end of the story; it was just the beginning, which brings us back to where we started, to America's next crossroad. In the past, tyrants, tyranny, and intolerance had been the norm for most of the world's population, but now they represent isolated pockets. In the past, the rule of law, the way of liberty, and the hand of tolerance were in the minority, while today they are so much more prevalent, thanks to all that is good and right about America and its allies around the world. But sadly, since the dark days of the 1960s, in the aftermath of JFK's assassination, the Vietnam War, and Watergate, the American landscape is awash with a terrible enemy: that enemy is cynicism.

Cynicism can best be defined as the tendency to always question the actions of others, no matter how honest or good they appear to be outwardly. The cynic, even in the face of evidence to the contrary, will always assume others have an ulterior motive, which is said to be a secret desire for money, prestige, and power, rather than intending it for the goodwill of others. As such, the cynic cares little for the historical facts surrounding the incredible strides that America has made on issues like the abolition of slavery, the suffrage of women, and the more humane treatment of our animal counterparts. So it will always be with the corrosive power of the cynical mind.

And so, here we are, as a nation of law, liberty, and tolerance, standing at a crossroad, on the verge of choosing yet another direction in the course of our storied history. If Providence prevails, as it has always prevailed, the direction we take as a nation will no doubt make us even more of what we have always been destined to become. But make no mistake, we'll never get to where we need to be by succumbing to the crippling cynicism that threatens our country today.

We need an antidote, then, for this disease, which is currently eroding every level of our society. Widespread cynicism has many people criticizing our most important institutions, from our government, to our educational system, from our families, to our houses of worship. They are being criticized because they're said to be, among other things, racist, misogynist, and intolerant, and therefore they must be dismantled. According to the critics, nothing short of an outright revolution is required.

The problem with such demands, though, is they overlook a critical aspect of the discussion, which is that while institutions are made up of people, institutions themselves aren't capable of racism, misogyny, or intolerance. Only people are capable of that. And as we all know from our own experience, not everyone is guilty of such things, just some. Some people are racist, some people are misogynist, some people are intolerant; that is without question. So to insist on dismantling institutions that have served not only America but the world on the presumed basis that they're racist, misogynist, or intolerant seems to miss the point entirely. Far better to seek reformation of the things that can be reformed, the things which comprise these institutions, which is to say, people.

It is also worth noting that Jesus was no fan of revolutions "from without" or else He'd have toppled the Roman Empire Himself, as the Jews in His day had been hoping and praying for. He did, however, revolutionize it "from within," one person at a time. That's why the American Revolution succeeded, as it first originated from within, then grew into a coalition of thirteen colonies that eventually formed a uniquely singular identity. Of course, without France's help, the Revolution would have failed. But who would argue that it was the French who imposed their will on the colonies to secede?

Even now, when America tries to steer other countries toward a republican form of government, from without, things don't always turn out so well. That's because unless the Lord builds the house—from within, beginning with one human heart at a time—the builders build in vain.

But rather than demand that people change, the critics insist that America itself must change, or else be changed. However, in doing so, they reveal they don't really have the best interests of America and the world in mind. Something altogether different, then, is lurking within their zealous cries of racism, misogyny, and intolerance. Everywhere we turn, we see our most basic values as a nation being questioned in a non-stop effort to undermine the American way of life.

Taking a page from God's own playbook—although a counterfeit version—the enemies of America have taken a new approach in their revolutionary effort. Rather than attack America in a head-on assault, they too are seeking to do their work from the inside out. But instead of appealing to "the better angels of our nature," they're pumping their favorite poison into every stream of public and private life: cynicism. Speaking of this very method of attack, President Lincoln predicted long ago:

> At what point then is the approach of danger to be expected? I answer, if it ever reaches us, it must spring up amongst us. It cannot come from abroad. If destruction be our lot, we must ourselves be its author and finisher. As a nation of freemen, we must live through all time, or die by suicide.[7]

Observations like this are vital to a work of this nature, because while it's presented with an acute awareness of the political upheaval of the day, it's by no means a political treatise about revolution, any more than it's a psychological treatise about cynicism. This is, after all, a work about the prayer of Jesus that urges the God of Heaven to have His will be done on Earth. It's about that expanding Empire—the coming of God's Kingdom that the prophets of old spoke of and that Jesus sent into full swing with His death and resurrection. And it's about the role that America, technology, and the New Earth are playing in this unfolding drama of the ages. So, while both the politics and the psychology of the day are relevant to this discussion, they will never constitute its main thrust.

---

7   *From a speech to a group in Springfield, Illinois 1838*

The main thrust of this work will be what *The Bible* says about the promises that God has uttered concerning His nation, a people whom the Lord has called by His name. It's especially about those promises, of the unconditional kind, that God intends to keep regardless of our typically human tendency to fail to live up to those promises. That's because no discussion of America—its birth, its history, and its destiny—can ever be understood apart from looking at it through the prism of a biblical perspective. Because no matter how long and how hard the critics of America question the motives of its founders, including Columbus, the Pilgrims, and the Founding Fathers, all these pioneers looked to *The Bible* for inspiration. And one promise they were all aware of, and one that Lincoln almost certainly had in mind when he offered the previous warning, was:

> "No weapon forged against you will prosper, and you'll refute every tongue that accuses you. This is the heritage of the servants of the Lord, and this is their vindication from Me," declares the Lord.[8]

This is worth remembering when America's problems so often concern outside forces generated by foreign nationals who seek to destabilize and destroy our way of life. But with God's unconditional promises such as this one, we can and should focus our attention on where it's required most: not on any enemy without but, rather, on the enemy within.

Keep in mind that as troublesome as bombs or missiles are, coming at us from beyond our borders, the greater threat is the one that can hide in plain sight, the one where you're never quite sure about its origins. After all, who needs bombs and missiles when a daily diet of nationwide cynicism has its own citizens undermining the foundations of its own institutions? Who needs physical weapons when we lay down and die of our own accord because someone has convinced us that we're to blame for the decadence and decline of our own nation? Like a cancer cell that must first trick its host into believing that it's part of the original organism, cynicism is insinuating itself into every organ of the once-stable national order of America.

---

8   Isaiah 54:17

But fortunately, for our sakes, the remedy for cynicism is as close to us as it's always been—in our collective memory as a society. Like Dorothy's ruby red slippers in *The Wizard of Oz*, the answer has always been with us, had we not become so jaded about the answer. When the power of cynicism seeks to poison every aspect of our national life, we should seek to remember.

Remember what the prophet Isaiah said, speaking for God:

> Listen to Me, you who pursue righteousness, you who seek the Lord: Look to the rock from which you were cut, and to the quarry from which you were hewn. Look to Abraham your father, and to Sarah who gave you birth. When I called him, he was but one; then I blessed him and multiplied him.[9]

To help with that remembering, this work will trace the history of Abraham, from the days when he was but one, to the days when his descendants would fulfill God's promise to become so numerous that they could only be compared with the dust of the Earth and the stars of Heaven.[10] Who are these people in today's modern world? Where in the world do they reside in order to contain so vast a population? And most importantly, did God fulfill His promise to multiply these people because they're more righteous than any other nation on Earth?

Certainly, answering such questions won't be easy. But just as certainly, we have no doubt that the antidote we need has everything to do with remembering what God's word says concerning the destiny of these dust-like descendants of Israel.

In this instance, that remembering can come to us—if we're willing to look to the quarry from which we were cut—just as it came to another famous group who once faced their own crossroad in history. The group in question was none other than those outcasts and wanderers in the days of Moses who had led them for forty years through the Wilderness. Now they were on the verge of entering the Promised Land. But before Moses handed them off to Joshua, he left them with one final admonition that history records as *The Song of Moses*. What he told them in that

---

9   Isaiah 51:1-2

10   Genesis 13:16; 15:5

fateful moment is the same thing our American ancestors took to heart in their day, and we'd do well to take it to heart in ours. Said Moses:

> Isn't God your Father and Creator? Didn't He make you and establish you? Remember the days of old; consider the years long past. Ask your fathers, and they'll tell you, your elders, and they'll inform you. When the Most High divided their inheritance to the nations, and when He separated the sons of Adam, He set the boundaries of the peoples according to the number of the Children of Israel. But the Lord's portion is His people, Jacob is His allotted inheritance.[11]

When the Pilgrims made the impossible voyage from the Old World to the New, they looked to Scriptures like this to shine a beacon of hope, to light their way in their darkest hour. For them, the idea that God had already determined the boundaries of the Children of Israel renewed their strength and courage when they needed it most. As fellow outcasts and wanderers, they found the parallels between those Israelites and themselves compelling and downright inspirational. Little did they know that the connection between these two groups, separated by so many centuries, was more than coincidental. In fact, with the benefit of hindsight, we now know just how connected they truly are: a connection which just happens to constitute a dimension of the antidote that I'll be offering in the pages of this work.

But to fully grasp what I mean by that, I'd first encourage everyone interested in partaking of this much-needed antidote to take Moses' advice:

> Remember the days of old; consider the years long past. Ask your fathers, and they'll tell you, your elders, and they'll inform you.

Most importantly for the purposes of this work concerning the borders of the Children of Israel, let's also remember what Jesus said, in *The Gospel of Matthew*, that the Kingdom of God was being taken from the Jews of His day and was being giv-

---

11   Deuteronomy 32:6-9

en to a nation that would bear fruit.[12] Knowing as we do of God's promise to bless the world through the descendants of Abraham, through Isaac and Jacob,[13] we again have to ask: Who among these dust-like peoples—the allotted inheritance of the Lord—qualifies for such a blessing? And where are they now?

Again, I say: Ask your fathers; they'll inform you.

And remember...

---

12   Matthew 21:43
13   Genesis 28:14

CHAPTER ONE

A FIRM FOUNDATION

*They won't hurt or destroy in all My holy
mountain: for the Earth will be full of the
knowledge of the Lord, as the waters cover the sea.
(Isaiah 11:19)*

Wanderers and Outsiders

WHENEVER you hope to build something of lasting value, it's always wise to build it on a firm foundation. That's why I've built this work, *On Earth as It is On Heaven*, on the foundation of the first two books I've written, namely *Tales of Forever* and *Fish Tales (From the Belly of the Whale)*.

If you've already read them, then all the better, because those who have will be better equipped to receive my conclusions in this work. However, even if you haven't read them, hopefully what I'll describe here will prepare you to receive them.

As for *Tales of Forever*, the first key takeaway is how it establishes a clear pattern of God's word being given to humanity, of that knowledge being lost, then of it being found again after a "set time" of punishment has expired.

This pattern of "lostness" is one in which God bestows His wisdom through His chosen messengers, but because of complacency and pride that message is, over time, taken for granted and marginalized, so God removes that knowledge from the

Earth as a wakeup call.

Then after a specified period of time has run its course, which usually corresponds to the time humanity had been gifted with that wisdom, there's a time of rediscovery and reawakening, with the next group being afforded the opportunity to succeed where the previous group failed.

This happened in *The Old Testament* period when *The Bible* was lost during the Babylonian Captivity, until Ezra, like Enoch long before him, miraculously authored the books that then restored its lost contents.[14]

And it happened again in *The New Testament* period when *The Bible*, as we presently know it, was "lost" during the Dark Ages when it was imprisoned in Latin so that only a cadre of elites could read it, until John Wycliffe in 1381 began the process of translating it into the language of the common people.

By 1387 Dutch lay preachers called Lollards, which means "wanderers" in Dutch, were roaming the English countryside, inspired by Wycliffe's belief that everyone deserved the opportunity to read God's word for themselves, and not just a handful of cloistered scholars.

By the way, the idea that "wanderers," or "outsiders" as they were deemed by the mainstream, spearheaded the great awakenings in biblical history is one of the cornerstones of this book, as we'll see throughout this work.

The next key takeaway from *Tales of Forever*, which feeds directly into the main thesis of *On Earth*, is that the dramatic narratives of *The Bible* reveal a truth far more potent than the typical view of Scripture as being a mere guide to right and wrong modes of human behavior.

Therefore, *Tales of Forever* seeks to establish an awareness of the role of biblical typology, in which we see how the stories of the patriarchs don't just record the lives of folks who encountered God and who had various reactions to those encounters.

Instead, when we look at the whole record of Scripture, we see how God entered into the very lives of these people to weave a tapestry for the sake of an onlooking world. In short, Scripture doesn't just record random stories, here and there; instead,

---

14 *Second Esdras 14:21-22, 24-27, 44-48*

it tells the stories of lesser messianic figures like Enoch, Noah, Abraham, Isaac, Moses, Joshua, and David in such a way that they foreshadow the role that the ultimate messianic person, Jesus Christ, plays in God's redemptive plan for humanity.

As such, the life of Abraham doesn't just tell the story of someone who was lucky enough to have God single him out, talk to him, and rescue him from a life of wandering aimlessly about. In the context of biblical typology, Abraham was a stand-in for all humanity who are in a far worse condition than any of us cares to admit.

Thus, in response to God's audacious promises, Abraham asked: "How will I know, Lord, that You're telling me the truth? Not that I doubt You, but because I doubt myself, because I doubt my worthiness to receive such wonderful promises as You're describing."

So how did God respond to Abraham when he asked for evidence—as any sane person would—that He wasn't hallucinating? God gave Abraham—and all of us—a marvelous way to verify the truthfulness of His promises. He told him:

> Certainly you'll know I'm telling you the truth when you see how I treat your descendants in the days to come, when you see them wandering for many years as strangers in a strange land. Then after becoming slaves, they'll suffer terribly at the hands of their overlords, but in the fourth generation, they'll come out richer than when they went in.[15]

The important thing to understand about this scenario, to those who appreciate God's habit of typological revelation: This wasn't just a way to confirm God's word to Abraham when He promised him descendants as numerous as the stars, and the gift of land previously owned by others. It was also a window into the human condition, of which Abraham and his descendants would act as surrogates for all peoples and for all time. In other words, God wasn't just promising Abraham a marvelous destiny for his sake alone but for the sake of every living human being—past, present, and future.

------

15   *Genesis 15:13-15*

That is to say, God would work out a universal mystery, in Abraham, that actually began when Adam fell from grace and was cast out of the Garden as the first "wanderer" and "outsider." Originally acting as the master of God's creation, Adam became a slave of Satan, and so was doomed to wander the Earth as a stranger in a strange land. But fortunately, because God is both a God of mercy and a God of "set times," the times of divine punishment are not eternal in nature.

Now, without going too deep at this point, I mention this in passing to make one important point, which is to confirm the pattern in Scripture, of God's consistent habit of periodically removing His blessings from mankind but then just as consistently restoring those blessings right on time. If you reject this, however, if you reject that God provides humanity with signposts as to His times of punishment and restoration, then you'll certainly reject the main thesis of this work. On the other hand, if you do acknowledge this timeless pattern of "give and take," then you'll be perfectly attuned to the idea that biblical figures like Abraham really do act as God's type for humanity.

In Abraham's case, although he faithfully embraced God's call by leaving his father's home en route to an undiscovered country, that state of having been "called out" didn't immediately deliver him from the foibles of human nature. Till the day he died, Abraham wrestled with the same state of spiritual ignorance, alienation, and slavery that haunts us all whether we realize it or not. Contrary to church tradition, which wants to declare Abraham an instant saint, he still failed many times in his journey of faith; he lied repeatedly—to himself and to others—even though from his point of view he was just trying "to help" God keep His promises. But in the end, despite God's imputation of righteousness for his faith, Abraham was still a slave to death, Hell, and the grave, until such time as Christ broke asunder that condition into which every human has been born ever since Adam was exiled from the Garden.

Concerning this interplay between ignorance and enlightenment, between alienation and restoration, between slavery and freedom, we'll have more to say as we continue in this work.

Paradoxes and Misconceptions

AS FOR the key takeaway from *Fish Tales (From the Belly of the Whale)*, toward a better understanding of *On Earth*, it's critical that we gain the tools to read *The Bible* so as to make our own conclusions free of the traditions of mankind. And when I say mankind, I also mean to say free of the traditions of the Church. Now in saying that, I'm not saying that *all* the traditions of the Church should be rewritten; I'm only saying that if you read *The Bible* for yourself, then you can't help but be struck by certain inconsistencies.

Now sometimes, as I've explained in *Fish Tales*, these aren't so much inconsistencies as they are paradoxes, which are there by God's design and are clear expressions of the paradoxical nature of the Divine. However, there are many verses in *The Bible* that after further review constitute genuine inconsistencies and so are really misconceptions of *The Bible*.

What's the difference, then, between a paradox and a misconception? Examples of a paradox are when Jesus is called the Prince of Peace,[16] but elsewhere in Scripture He said, "I haven't come to bring peace but to bring a sword."[17] Or when Jesus said, "Seek and you'll find,"[18] but elsewhere He said, "Whoever seeks to save his life will lose it, but whoever loses his life for My sake will save it."[19] By definition a paradox is something that at first glance seems incongruous but turns out to be true when we take the time to reconcile the paradoxical nature of the verses in question.

In contrast, a misconception is when a traditional reading of Scripture contains an obvious contradiction, and no matter how much we try to reconcile that view with the rest of Scripture, it still can't be done.

Take for example how *The Bible* has Jesus telling us: "Blessed are the meek, because they will inherit the Earth."[20] In this

---

16   Isaiah 9:6

17   Matthew 10:34

18   Ibid. 7:7

19   Luke 9:24; 17:33

20   Matthew 5:5

famous little verse, we have yet another classic case of why the Scriptures seem to be more a source of confusion than of clarity.

To begin with, we have the first half of this verse using a very misleading word, "meek," which has created all kinds of nonsense concerning what it means to be a real man or real woman of faith; then we have the second half, with the word "inherit," that's just as troublesome but for a completely different reason.

I mean, just consider how humanity has come to view the two keywords in this verse: "meek" and "inherit." Together they create an incredibly pathetic picture of what the God of *The Bible* seems to be looking for in populating His Kingdom. It's as though God put out a Help Wanted sign for eternity: "Calling all milquetoasts for Jesus, to do nothing all day long. Benefits, to inherit one Earth, to be discarded in favor of heavenly bliss."

To anyone who knows anything about what God is really looking for, what could be more irritating about the traditional interpretation of this verse?

Fortunately, as is the case with all biblical misconceptions, the antidote is as near as any Greek and Hebrew Dictionary. I prefer *Strong's Exhaustive Concordance of The Bible*. Let's see what it helps us to see. This word "meek" is translated from the Greek word, *praus*, which doesn't at all describe someone who is timid or feeble, as we've been led to believe by any traditional view of this word. The word *praus* actually describes the taming of the wild horses that were used in the Roman Coliseum.

Prior to the Romans, the Greeks would capture wild horses that then needed to be trained for battle. Only those horses that would allow a master to control them were found suitable. Contrary to the modern idea of meekness, then, Jesus isn't talking about powder-puffs or doormats in this verse but powerful ones who are no longer rebellious or unruly; war horses that can now stride into battle without breaking rank or panicking under fire.

It is this type of man or woman, actually, who is destined to inherit the Earth, not by sitting around and praying to die so they can go to Heaven. It's this type who willingly accepts the proverbial "bit" in their mouth, under the guidance of their rider, and who wages war with the prince of this world and thereby reclaims the dominion forfeited so long ago in the Garden.

What's more, this word "inherit" gives the impression that this inheritance will be what we typically think of, in which the "meek" will be receiving the gift of the Earth as a mere by-product of someone else's death. In short, we do absolutely nothing but wait around until somebody dies and, poof, we get all the goodies. But not so when you look more closely at the Hebrew word used in this verse for this word "inherit."

In *The Old Testament*, the word is used in the context of the Israelites taking possession of the Promised Land, as in when they were told to destroy the inhabitants of Canaan and possess Palestine, now that the "fullness of the Amorites was complete." To those who appreciate biblical typology, the parallel is clear: Just as the Israelites in Moses' day had to dispossess the people who were already there, the people of Jesus' day were told they had to dispossess those who were under the devil's dominion and who had thus, from God's view, been squatters since the day Adam forfeited his gift of the Earth.

What I find most interesting in all of this is, as long as I can remember, this verse always gave me the impression that if these so-called "meek" ones had any hope of inheriting anything involving the Earth, it spoke more of the New Earth than of the present Earth. I say that because, again, the traditional view makes us believe there's nothing anyone can do to withstand the forces of Anti-Christ in the Last Days, so our only hope now is to be rescued via the Rapture thereby triggering the final march to Armageddon. In other words, so much credit is given to the enemies of God and His Church, there isn't much hope of inheriting anything but a scorched, post-apocalyptic Earth as depicted in so many sci-fi works of fiction.

At which point I'd suggest that perhaps we're investing way too much energy into something that Jesus isn't even talking about. After all, what can the Church possibly do to inherit the New Earth in the context just described as dispossessing the prior inhabitants thereof? Yes, the seven nations of Canaan were already there before Joshua led Israel into action; and yes, the nations of the New World were already there before the Great Commission of Christ compelled men like Columbus to act. But certainly no one believes there will be anyone occupying the

New Earth who needs to be dispossessed, do they?

Bottom line: Only when we're willing to let the whole of God's word speak for itself can we finally embrace the truth of Scripture in spite of all the clamoring, haranguing voices that seek to refute the still, small voice of God.

As the Waters Cover the Sea

NOW, AS for the biblical misconceptions we'll be addressing in *On Earth as It is On Heaven*, we'll ask whether or not:

Christ asked us to honor Him by praying "The Lord's Prayer," repeatedly and publicly, until His return.

The disciples were on board with the simple prayer of Jesus, in regard to God's coming Kingdom upon the Earth, and to His gift of daily bread and forgiveness.

The goal of every Christian is to die and go to Heaven.

Despite Adam and Eve's fall from grace, humans are still—legally speaking—masters of creation.

Despite the Fall of Man, God is still—legally speaking—the master of humanity.

Ever since the final days of *The New Testament*, God is no longer in the business of performing miracles, choosing and guiding nations, or intervening in the lives of individuals.

America isn't special and therefore it's wrong to think of itself as being unique among nations, in the history of nations.

America can be deemed legitimate only if it was born in perfection—perfection in morality, perfection in liberty, and perfection in equality.

The New World, as epitomized in the land called America, was merely accidental and incidental in God's overall plan to evangelize the world with the Gospel of Christ.

America began in 1492, with the discovery of America by Christopher Columbus, or in 1620, with the landing at Plymouth Rock by the Pilgrims, or in 1776, with the signing of the Declaration of Independence by the Founding Fathers.

The promise to Abraham and his descendants concerning their becoming like the stars of the sky, and their becoming a company of nations are to be interpreted in strictly spiritual terms, as opposed to their being fulfilled in physical terms.

The promise to Abraham and his descendants that they would be a blessing to the whole world speaks only in regard to a heavenly blessing and not an earthly blessing.

The promise to David and his descendants about their sitting upon a perpetual throne that is to endure like the Sun and the Moon can only be fulfilled by Jesus Christ as the eternal Son of God.

The promise to David through Nathan about God preparing a place where Israel might dwell without being attacked by her ancient enemies is not to be understood in historical terms but is really speaking of Christ's throne in eternity.

The Western technology that created a worldwide web of electronic-based telecommunications was merely accidental and incidental in God's overall plan to evangelize the world with the Gospel of Christ.

The Earth is alien to all things in Heaven.

The human body is alien to all things in Heaven.

The Kingdom of God is alien to all things on Earth.

And finally, the Stone Kingdom, described by the prophet Daniel, can only be fulfilled beyond history, and on the New Earth, as opposed to being fulfilled in history, and on the present Earth.

All this and more will be examined as we delve into the worldview that *The Bible* conveys. More often than not, though, traditions are so entrenched that even the most ardent believer has a difficult time separating what Scripture says from what it doesn't say.

If that's true, then by all means let us focus less on what would distract us from the context of God's word of truth, and focus more on the entire narrative of *The Bible*, from front to back. Let's focus less on escaping this "wheel of life," as is suggested by "otherworldly" philosophies, as though there's nothing of this life or this Earth worth salvaging. Instead, let's focus more on dispossessing the personifications of evil who'd rather see God's magnificent creation turned over to the buzzards and hyenas. Let's carry on with the work that Jesus' disciples were charged with when Christ gave them the keys of God's Kingdom, and in turn were charged with gifting them to us. Let's take it to heart that God's Earth and all its fullness is never to be discarded in favor of "greener pastures" over yonder, and that all evil needs to win is for good people to do nothing.

And so with all of the preceding thoughts in mind, let's take aim at what the title of this work could mean, in spite of every human tradition that would confuse us about the true destiny of God's nation and the Earth, of which Isaiah, the prophet, spoke:

> They won't hurt or destroy in all My holy mountain: for the Earth will be full of the knowledge of the Lord, as the waters cover the sea.[21]

---

21 *Isaiah 11:9*

CHAPTER TWO

A STILL SMALL VOICE

*Then the Lord said, "Pay attention, Elijah,
because the Lord is about to pass by." And
a mighty wind tore into the mountains and
shattered the rocks, but the Lord wasn't in the
wind. After the wind there came an earthquake,
but the Lord wasn't in the earthquake. After the
earthquake came a fire, but the Lord wasn't in the
fire. And after the fire came a still, small voice.
(First Kings 19:9-12)*

In His Wildest Dreams

AMERICA, technology, and the New Earth—three things that, at first glance, don't seem to have any direct connection. Granted, America and technology have intersected on more than one occasion, but what could they possibly have in common with the New Earth as it's described in *The Bible*? What's more, how have all three of these seemingly disconnected subjects found themselves clustered together under the main title of this work: *On Earth as It is On Heaven*?

"And pardon me for stating the obvious," you may add, "but isn't there a typo in your title? Don't you mean to say, on Earth as it is 'in' Heaven, and not 'on' Heaven?"

To which I'd reply: "Actually, no, I haven't erred in my intention when I speak of those things that are 'on' Heaven as opposed to their being 'in' Heaven. And to explain what I mean by that, let me offer the following explanation."

In weaving a story with multiple elements—of America, of technology, of the New Earth, and of being "on" Heaven instead of "in" it—we have to address a series of questions that depend on *The Bible* to adequately answer them. First ask yourself: When you think of how the God of *The Bible* acts, what do you usually think of?

Some people think of God parting the Red Sea with a blast of His nostrils, while others imagine Him creating Heaven and Earth from out of nothing. Some think of God raising Jesus from the dead, while others see Him swooping up Elijah in a whirlwind of fire and smoke. Still others think of God breathing life into Adam and creating a human being, while some picture Him raining fire and brimstone down upon Sodom and Gomorrah. In short, when we think of how God acts, we typically think of Him doing things that only God can do, either in terms of what He does or is said to be, such as His being omnipotent, omniscient, and omnipresent.

But the most overlooked aspect of how God acts is the way He sometimes does things quite differently from what we expect Him to do; sometimes God acts as though He isn't God at all. A prime example of the contrast between how we expect God to act and how we don't expect Him to act is found in the nineteenth chapter of *The First Book of Kings*. There, Elijah, the prophet, is fleeing the wrath of Jezebel after Ahab told her how Elijah had killed all the prophets of Baal.

> So Jezebel sent a message to Elijah: "May the gods deal with me, and ever so severely, if by this time tomorrow I don't make your life like the lives of those you killed!"
>
> And Elijah was afraid and ran for his life. When he came to Beersheba in Judah, he left his servant there, while he himself traveled a day's journey into the wilderness. He sat down under a broom tree and prayed that he might die. "I've had enough, Lord," he said. "Take my life, because I'm no better than my fathers."[22]

---

22 *First Kings 19:1-5*

Then, trying to get as far away from Jezebel as he could, Elijah traveled a great distance where he found a nice cave to hide in. But no sooner had he settled in for the night than the Word of the Lord came and asked, "Elijah, what are you doing here?"

"I've been very zealous for the Lord, the God of Hosts," he replied, "but the Israelites have forsaken Your covenant, torn down Your altars, and killed Your prophets with the sword. I'm the only one left, and now they're seeking my life as well."

Then the Lord said, "Go out and stand on the mountain before the Lord. Pay attention, Elijah, because the Lord is about to pass by."

And a mighty wind tore into the mountains and shattered the rocks, but the Lord wasn't in the wind.

After the wind came an earthquake, but the Lord wasn't in the earthquake.

After the earthquake came a fire, but the Lord wasn't in the fire.

And after the fire came a still, small voice.[23]

It was then that God reassured Elijah that he wasn't alone in his fight with Ahab and Jezebel; there were yet 7,000 men whom God had reserved in Israel who hadn't pledged their allegiance to Baal.[24]

The great irony of this scene, in which Elijah fled the wrath of Jezebel, is we'd expect that, after everything he saw God do up till then, Elijah would never have been so afraid of Jezebel's death threat. After all, in response to Elijah's faithfulness, God, just one chapter earlier in *First Kings*, had famously rained fire down from Heaven to consume his offering before all the people.

So Elijah said to everyone there, "Come near to me." And they all came closer to him... Elijah then took twelve stones according to the number of the tribes of the sons of Jacob, to whom the Word of the Lord had come, saying, "Israel will be your name." And he built

---

23 *First Kings 19:9-12*

24 *Ibid. 19:18*

an altar with the stones, in the name of the Lord, and he made a trench around the altar, large enough to hold two measures of seed.

Then he arranged the wood and cut an ox in pieces as a burnt offering and laid it on the wood. And he said, "Fill four pitchers with water and pour it on the burnt offering and on the wood." And he said, "Do it a second time," and they did it a second time. And he said, "Do it a third time," and they did it a third time. The water flowed around the altar and he also filled the trench with water.

At the time of the offering of the evening sacrifice, Elijah, the prophet, came near and said, "Oh Lord, God of Abraham, Isaac, and Israel, today let it be known that You are God in Israel, and that I'm Your servant and I've done all these things at Your word. Answer me, oh Lord, answer me, so this people may know that You, oh Lord, are God, and that You have turned their hearts back again."

Then the fire of the Lord fell and consumed the burnt offering and the wood and the stones and the dust, and licked up the water that was in the trench.[25]

Just when Elijah needed it most, God acted like only God could act. Strangely, though, it still did nothing to ensure that Elijah wouldn't doubt God's ability to protect him from Jezebel's subsequent lust for revenge. So what did God do when Elijah's faith wavered? He came to His rescue again, of course.

But this time, the Lord came not only to help him but also to teach him—and us—a unique lesson. The arrival of the Lord brought with it a mighty wind, an earthquake, and a fire. Naturally, having just seen God's fiery power rain down on his burnt offering, Elijah would've assumed that all these things might bring him the solution he required. But no, it was the still, small voice that he really needed, although he might never have thought so in his wildest dreams.

Now admittedly, it's easy to criticize such inconsistencies in

---

the behavior of someone even as great as Elijah—in hindsight, that is—as no doubt none of us would've acted any differently than him. It could even be said this is why *The Bible* is such an enduring classic, because despite every criticism that it's flawed, by virtue of it being a written record of our distant past, it's never ceased in its ability to speak to our immediate present.

In short, *The Bible* provides us with a never-ending litmus test in our ongoing attempts to solve the riddle of why God acts the way He does. Again and again, the Scriptures declare that while many people saw God's actions, very few came to understand why He did what He did. As it is written: "God made known His ways to Moses, His deeds to the people of Israel."[26] In other words, the people of Israel only saw God's actions and therefore understood God only on a surface level, like children who see what their parents do but never really understand why they do what they do. Moses, by contrast, came to know God's ways; he came to know why God did what He did, and therefore He understood God on a much deeper level. Unlike the other kids in the family, Moses came to know why God acts the way He does, and as a result, he was much better able to anticipate and predict how God would act in future situations.

Since the Curtain Fell

IT IS precisely this kind of awareness that I'm seeking to investigate in this present work. That's why I'm asking the question: When we think of how the God of *The Bible* acts, what do we usually think of? Whether we consider ourselves a believer or a skeptic, this question is of paramount importance. In either case, we can't help but be perplexed by the apparent inconsistencies we encounter in *The Bible*. But if we can come to a better way of interpreting God's actions, we may come to a clearer understanding of many of our most pressing issues as a society, such as: If we consider that nations endure while individuals come and go, does that mean God is more concerned with the destiny of nations than of individuals? And just how relevant are the actions of a single person in the overall scheme of God's

---

26 Psalm 103:7

plan? After all, while God obviously revealed Himself to men like Moses and Elijah, isn't it true that God was more concerned with the fate of nations like Israel and Judah?

With Scripture as our reference point, it appears as though, while God is, and always will be, the Lord of the Nations, He understands all too well that nations can't respond to His still, small voice; only individuals can do that. Nations can't yearn for truth, freedom, and justice; only individuals can do that. Nations can't strive to live according to the rule of law and the liberty of conscience; only individuals can do that. And if that's true, then it turns out that, paradoxically, the individuals who comprise the nations—those puny individuals who come and go so swiftly—are, and always will be, the foundation upon which even the most enduring nation is built.

That's also why the technology of a nation is so critical in the overall scheme of God's plan—first, because the power of technology enables individuals to rise above the more mundane aspects of society that has characterized so much of world history; second, because each innovation in technology gives those individuals greater opportunity to spread their acquired knowledge to more people than ever before; and third, because technology is rarely the product of groupthink but, rather, is the brainchild of gifted individuals who bring to bear all that they've distilled from the society in which they've been nurtured and trained.

Be that as it may, while many who claim to believe in *The Bible* have no problem with God's still, small voice speaking to the prophets of old, they still can't help wondering: Is this method of divine communication still relevant in a modern setting? After all, it's been contended that since the curtain fell on the days described in *The Book of Acts*, God no longer takes an active part in the destiny of individuals or nations. Whereas God performed signs and wonders on behalf of biblical nations like Judah and Israel, those days are long gone, never to return again. Right?

Of course, if we believe in Scripture, we're forced to anticipate some kind of future manifestation of God's intervention on behalf of Judah and Israel because clearly they're major players in *The Book of Revelation*. Therefore, the question should be rephrased, and more importantly, rephrased in the context of this ebb and flow of God's way of doing things. Simply put: From those days described in *Acts* until the days in *Revelation*, has God "gone underground," as it were? After the nations of Judah and Israel failed so miserably to live up to God's call, did God stop guiding the destiny of individuals or nations? And if by chance He hasn't stopped, which individuals and nations is He still guiding?

Ironically enough, if *The Bible* remains our touchstone, we have to agree that God has never abandoned His habit of choosing certain individuals or nations to fulfill His purposes on the stage of world history. The only questions that remain, then: Are there clues that point to such individuals or nations? And if there are clues, then how do we account for this interplay of God sometimes acting in obvious ways, while at other times acting inconspicuously?

CHAPTER THREE

OUTSIDERS LOOKING IN

*"You are My witnesses," declares the Lord,
"and My servant whom I've chosen, so
that you may consider and believe Me and
understand that I am He… I am the Lord,
your Holy One, the Creator of Israel, and your
King." So says the Lord Who makes a way in
the sea and a path through the surging waters.
(Isaiah 43:10, 15-16)*

Postcards From Heaven

EVER HEARD the saying: Some people are so heavenly minded, they're no earthly good? Just ask that sort: "What's the most important message in *The Bible*? I mean, sure, it's a book about faith, hope, and love, about Christ dying for our sins, about receiving forgiveness for those sins and finding the road to eternal life. I get that. But apart from that: What is it about *The Bible* that lets us know it's more than just a nice story with a happy ending? Isn't *The Bible* supposed to contain a message of *why* all the things like faith, forgiveness, and eternal life are possible? Isn't it supposed to demonstrate that God is in control, and that because He's in control, He can be trusted to keep His promises to humanity?"

If God is like the Deists tell us, then sure, He made the Universe, wound it up like a clock, and set all the laws of the

Universe into motion. But after that, if He checked out and left the Universe to mankind, then there's no evidence that He's in control of anything that's important to us, as in, the destiny of the nations of the world or the people who make up those nations. If He isn't in control of the nations or us, then all this talk of faith, hope, and love is out the window. It's meaningless, because even if God built into the Universe the free will of every living entity, it doesn't mean He's a God Who can be trusted.

"But of course God can be trusted," insist the sincere believers in Scripture. "Of course God is in control."

At which point, one quite naturally asks for some tangible proof of God's control over history, over the nations, over us.

But instead of hearing about this proof from Scripture itself, we're offered only platitudes, like: "Well, you just have to trust that He's in control; that's all there is to it. When you see nation rising up against nation, when you hear of wars and rumors of wars, when there are earthquakes, famines, and pestilences in many places, you're not supposed to see confusion and disarray in all that; you're supposed to see that God is in control. Right?"

To which I'd reply, "Oh, really, that's your proof? When we see disaster and chaos, we're supposed to see God's faithfulness to His word? Is that all there is to it, then?"

"Well, yes," comes the befuddled response. "I'm sorry I don't have a better answer for you, but that's all I've got, friend. But fear not, the Lord will restore all things someday, when He splits the sky and returns in all His glory. Till then, we have the hope of being made worthy in God's sight, the hope of eternal life, the hope of being received into Heaven after we die. Isn't that enough?"

To which I'd reply, "I suppose so, sure. The only problem with your train of thought is: If *The Bible* doesn't reveal the way in which God is in control, then what's the point of looking to it? What good is it if the tales of Scripture are nothing more than cheery postcards from Heaven, telling us to keep a stiff upper lip until God makes it all better someday? If *The Bible* doesn't provide us with evidence of God's control over history, then how do we know He controls our lives as individuals? If God isn't in control of our lives—in this mess of a world we call 'life'—then how can we trust Him? And if we can't trust Him, then how can we inherit this eternal life you speak of? Without trust, what are we to make of this thing you call hope?"

But what if there really is tangible evidence of God's control over history? What if that evidence involves more than a series of sporadic moments and disconnected events, as traditionally understood, in Scripture? What if it speaks of more than Adam and Eve's expulsion from the Garden of Eden? More than the Flood of Noah, and the Tower of Babel? The call and blessing of Abraham, Isaac, and Jacob? The exodus from Egypt, the conquest of Canaan, and the building of a Temple? The rise and fall of two mighty nations—Israel, to the north, and Judah, to the south? The life, the death, and the resurrection of Jesus of Nazareth?

And what if there is evidence that God never ceased controlling human history just because we're told the curtain dropped after those final acts in the days of *The New Testament*? That He's involved with more than the history of the Jewish people, as we've been led to believe? Or that there's more to biblical prophecy than what we're expecting in the pages of *The Book of Revelation*?

What if that evidence involves more than convincing people to pray so they can go to Heaven one day? What if it involves more nations of this world than tradition tells us? What if it involves the role that America has played, and is now playing, in history? Or how the technology of a world power like America has played, and is now playing? And what if *The Bible* provides evidence that the New World of yesterday is actually a shadow of things to come, of the New Earth that's said will one day appear as a beautiful bride adorned for her awaiting groom?

God the Outsider

NOW, in addressing the issue of God's intermittent actions, in which He sometimes acts in obvious ways, while at other times inconspicuously, we can't help but ask the most obvious question of all: If God is God, then why would there be any discrepancy in His actions in the first place? Doesn't *The Bible* tell us that God is the same yesterday, today, and forever? How, then, can we reconcile what is clearly a change in His behavior from age to age, year to year, and moment to moment?

Fortunately for us, we do have God's written answer to such questions, and in answering these questions, I'd first remind us of the most overlooked aspect of our present predicament. I'd suggest that it's not God Who is changing. Rather, the element of change has everything to do with us and our worldview. The confusion arises because, in searching the Scriptures for clues to our existence, we're incredibly prone to glossing over the most important clues that are there to help us understand how God and His ways impact that existence.

Take, for example, what I'd describe as one of the greatest cases of mistaken identity in the history of the human species. Take, for example, the opening book of *The Bible*, where God is said to have created humanity as His crowning achievement, and where it's said we're to rule and reign over the whole of creation. As such, God is to rule over the humans; humans are to rule over the animals; men are to rule over the women, etc., etc., etc. And ever since, we've seen a steady stream of chaos, in which one bunch is claiming they've been ordained to rule over the other bunch with all sorts of mixed results, generally not nearly as good as we'd expect if God was the One Who ordained it all.

So while skeptics and believers alike question God for the ensuing anarchy, the one to blame, I'd contend, isn't God but, rather, the humans who are incapable of thinking things through ever since that event *The Bible* calls the Fall of Man. And when I say this, I'm not trying to affirm the Calvinistic doctrine of the depravity of mankind, or the Catholic doctrine of original sin. Apart from the genuine implications of such thinking, I'm talking about an utter lack of logic when it comes to interpreting the message contained in the most foundational book of Scripture. In short, if humanity would accept the record of *Genesis* at face value, in the simple explanation it gives, many of the greatest misconceptions of *The Bible* would simply dissolve away into nothingness.

To reiterate: Why do God's various actions indicate that He's both everywhere and nowhere at the exact same time? The most obvious answer we obtain from *Genesis* is that while Adam and Eve were created in the image of the Divine, and so were possessors of freedom and self-determination, the choice that the first couple made in eating from the Tree of Knowledge severed the relationship that then existed between the natural and supernatural realms. As such, the shift from how the primordial world existed before the Fall of Man and what it became after that cataclysmic event can never in a million years be overstated. Though God was still God—still omniscient, still omnipotent, still omnipresent—humankind from that point on no longer partook of the same relationship.

Stop and think for a moment, if you will, what it might have been like living before the Fall, still living in the fullness of God's image, in a world still untainted by sadness or pain, slavery or suffering, darkness or death. Before the Fall, Adam and Eve were living in the same world as the Divine, but afterward, they were suddenly outsiders looking in, suddenly spiritual vagabonds dispossessed of freedom and self-determination. And so, just as Adam and Eve had become outsiders of God's world after the Fall, God likewise had become an outsider to their world—and ours—ever since. Again, the implications of this ontological truth have such immense ramifications that the human mind can barely grasp them without a great deal of contemplation and struggle.

Before the Fall, God was bound by a covenant that endued Adam and Eve with the divine presence which enveloped their very being. But after the Fall, God was equally bound by a covenant that revoked all that the divine presence bestowed upon them. That meant not only would disease, pain, and death enter into this new world of theirs, all of God's promises to them that they would rule and reign over the creation were revoked. Living in our modern age, in a world dominated by the scientific mastery of the elemental forces that surround us, this is something almost impossible for us to comprehend.

What's more, many believers of *The Bible* confuse the issue even further because they incorrectly insist humans are still lords and masters of creation by God's decree, despite the alteration of that decree as a result of the Fall. What we see, then, is that anyone who claims humanity still maintains the condition they possessed before the Fall is twisting history to fit their pet view of Scripture. That's because an honest appraisal of both the written record of *The Bible* and human history clearly demonstrates that after their expulsion from the Garden, Adam and Eve were no longer rulers over the elements of creation but slaves to them. No longer would they command the creation, the animals, and themselves; they were ever after prisoners of darkness and death, subject to the power and fear of the animals, and slaves and property of the devil to whom they submitted themselves when they defied God's command.

Worse still, it also meant that because God's covenant was voided by Adam and Eve's disobedience, God, the Outsider, was no longer the *legal* Lord and Master of humanity. No longer was God free to bestow His blessings upon them, not because He despised the apple of His eye or ceased to love them with an everlasting love, but because He is by nature a God of covenant—a God bound by His own honor and integrity, bound by His word of promise. That's why, from the moment the first couple was expelled from the Garden, they would be bound by a new covenant, and therefore their new *legal* lord and master was the devil himself, Satan.

Now keep in mind, when I say this, I'm not saying that this same God of covenant did not still have the power and desire to establish a new covenant for the sake of Adam and his descendants. Naturally, this is precisely what the story contained in Scripture was written to convey; the biblical record, then, is nothing less than the long and arduous road back to the presence of God, which road God alone provided the signposts in the various covenants that He's instituted by the mouth of His prophets. What I am saying, though, by all the authority contained in *The Bible* itself, is that what people have claimed about the exalted status of the human race is negated by a correct understanding of the difference between what God said about our status in the Universe before the Fall of Man, and what it has been ever since the days of Adam.

Unless this foundational truth is fully appreciated, we will never be able to understand why God acts the way He does in terms of the ages-long history of human redemption as depicted in Scripture. Unless we first settle this primary fact of human existence, we'll never come to appreciate that from the days of Adam to the time of the Great Flood, from the days of Noah until the time of the call of Abraham, and from the days of the Children of Israel until the days of the Advent of Christ, God has, by His own judicial decree, related to humanity as an outsider, outlier, and alien. This more than anything else explains why God sometimes acts in such godlike manner that no one dares question the divine nature of said actions, while at other times acts so inconspicuously that events can easily be dismissed as though no God at all was necessary for their occurrence.

It also explains why those chosen ones of God were, like Adam before them, the greatest outsiders of human history—men like Seth, Enoch, and Noah before the Flood, followed by the likes of Shem, Eber, and Abraham. The great constant running through the lives of the patriarchs was that all of them were never more alive than when they were embracing this peculiar sense of being "on the outside," while everyone else was content with being "on the inside." And in following the divine call, every one of them blazed a trail that enlarged God's expanding Empire and led the way for future generations to follow. Without the path uniquely cut by these lone wolves, there in turn could have been no Isaac or Israel or Judah; no Levi or Dan or Joseph; no Moses or Joshua or Caleb.

But long before men like Elijah stood outside the status quo, which led a chosen nation to turn its back on God, Adam set the stage for all the outsiders who would follow in his footsteps.

Turned Inside Out

HERE WE COME face to face with some of the greatest mysteries of all time: What was God thinking to even allow the devil an opportunity to deceive Adam and Eve? Could events have turned out differently? And considering the tragic results that humanity has experienced ever since, are we correct in assuming the Fall of Man is a failure in terms of the overall plan of God?

Fortunately, for all involved, what humans fear most, from our finite point of view, isn't the same thing at all from God's infinite point of view. From our temporal perspective, death and disease are abhorrent to us because we suffer at their hands on a personal level; however, from an eternal perspective, they achieve in the long run a much different end than we're capable of apprehending from our limited perspective.

As the story goes: God freely gave Adam dominion over the Earth and clearly outlined the prohibitions that were involved in that kingship. But rather than cooperate with God, Adam wasn't content with all that he'd been given. He wanted more, which was exactly what the devil was counting on, because it was this same attitude that had caused his downfall. Understanding this all too well, Satan masterfully exploited this fatal flaw, and by preying upon this weakness, he managed to entice Adam to follow his advice, thus beginning an entirely new chapter in humanity's existence.

But fortunately for us, God is capable of transcending any problem this Universe can throw at Him. In this case, God was faced with the outcome of Adam's disobedience, which resulted in him and his descendants being doomed to perpetual slavery to the world, the flesh, and the devil. But rather than spell the end of all of God's hopes for His created ones, God took the very thing with which Satan connived to thwart the divine plan and "turned it inside out," as it were.

Prior to the Fall, Adam and Eve knew only life and freedom in the Garden, but sadly, because of that peculiar condition, it also meant they were ignorant of the truth of what God warned them about when He said they'd die if they chose knowledge over trust. It was, therefore, only after the Fall that they'd ever learn the difference between the life that God had given them and the life they were confronted with after they forfeited it through their disobedience.

In short, the thing that God required of Adam and Eve was that they trust His word of promise, which they failed to do while yet in the Garden, primarily because, in their state of innocence, they had no way of knowing what disobedience would bring. Only afterward, then, could they begin the real journey of trusting God. But now, instead of trusting His word that spoke of death, while everything around them spoke only of life, they found themselves living in a mirror image of that first world. Whereas before they were ignorant of the consequences of not trusting God, they were suddenly in the unenviable position of knowing exactly why they needed to trust Him, though ironically it was because they presently lived as exiles from the direct presence of God as slaves of Satan—and, I might add, legally owned slaves at that.

However, though a life of servitude came as the price of freedom, the one redeeming aspect of this new existence was that God, as always, provided a unique way of transcending their dismal state. Whereas in that previous life of perpetual bliss, where God warned of death, the first couple now faced death all around them, even as God spoke of eternal life—if, that is, they'd act in accordance with the same kind of trust that was required of them before they were exiled.

In the end, then, the thing they could never have learned while still happily ensconced in their garden home would only become possible outside of it. Needless to say, this new life wasn't nearly as cozy and safe as their old life. But what it did bring them, which is to say, an everlasting connection to God, would eventually outweigh all that they'd temporarily lost in their fall from grace. So, just as the sacrifice of Christ turned death into something different from the way it began, so also the slavery of Adam was turned inside out. Only by facing one's own mortality can we discern our need of trusting God in a way that could never be achieved had such a state of existence not been allowed to overtake us. In this way, the slave status of the human race exists as a bittersweet condition, which works both against us and for us at the same time, much to the chagrin of the devil, I'm sure.

So, ironically, it would seem that subterfuge is as much a tactic for God as it is for the devil. Just think of how many centuries rolled by before Satan even had a clue that darkness, disease, and death might not be fulfilling his plan to destroy humanity. And even now, because the forces of Hell are incapable of seeing things the way God sees things, the devil and his minions are still by and large convinced they're winning the war against God's human creation.

A Hidden Path in the Sea

WHAT DO WE have so far, then? We began by asking: What connects America, technology, and the New Earth, in trying to explain how all three fall under the heading of things said to be "on" Heaven rather than "in" Heaven? To answer that, we introduced the idea that, while God typically acts as only God can act, His preferred method of acting is by way of His still, small voice, as demonstrated in the case of Elijah. That's because while the spectacular nature of God's miraculous deeds, like the parting of the Red Sea, can inspire awe and respect, it doesn't always communicate the same depth of awareness as does the articulate nature of God's word itself. This seems to explain why, although God often seems more interested in the destiny of nations, He acts on a more personal level than most might assume. Then when investigating the question of why God's actions ebb and flow in and out of view, we asked if this happens because God Himself is somehow changing, and so came to see this didn't happen because God was changing but, rather, because of the changing relationship that humans have in relation to the God of Covenants. In this way, we determined how God and humans now both exist, from a purely legal perspective, as outsiders looking into a world they once related to in a far different manner prior to the Fall of Man. And so it was that this more than anything else explains why God sometimes acts in conspicuous ways that are obvious to everyone, while at other times He acts inconspicuously and "under the radar," so to speak.

Simply put: The spectacular power of God, which is thus hidden away within the articulate power of a still, small voice, becomes the perfect vehicle to activate and guide God's chosen ones, which in turn localizes the presence of God via these individuals. These individuals then communicate what God has made known to them, which is either believed and embraced or disbelieved and rejected by others in their group who in turn create communities of belief or disbelief. This in turn sets the stage for the spawning of societies that in time create towns and cities, which mirror the beliefs of those individuals who founded them. These towns and cities then go on to provide the basis for what are called nation-states. Thus, the key to understanding world history depends on a correct view of who among the various nations is most effectively co-opting in the overall plan of God as it's described in the biblical record.

However, what we should never lose sight of is that the original building blocks for these larger national units are those smaller individual units which are themselves the receptacles for what is communicated by the still, small voice of God. As such, the more we come to appreciate the role of the individual in God's redemptive plan, the more we come to appreciate the role of a nation's technology to transmit the message communicated by the still, small voice. This in turn spawns the broadcasting of God's message, whether that message is communicated to a given nation where it presently exists or where that message is, for some specific reason, taken from its original recipients and rebroadcast somewhere else to another nation of God's choice. Upon closer inspection, then, the invention of new modes of transportation and communication will take on new meaning in the context of whom God assigns His stewardship, in terms of both His choice He's made presently clear, and His choice He's purposely hidden until some future date.

It is therefore within the context of these various elements that the story of the promise of America, technology, and the New Earth will next be told. More specifically, it's a story that involves a God Who is more concerned with those who cooperate with His still, small voice than those who expect Him to split the sea at every turn with a blast of His nostrils. So, while the Israelites of old saw the parting of the Red Sea yet failed to trust God ever after, in the case of America, the New World would be established by a people who were content with God's word guiding them, with neither fanfare nor notoriety, by way of a hidden path in the sea.

For Christopher Columbus that guidance came to him in 1492 when, on his first voyage of discovery, his crew warned him that if they continued one more day on their present course, he'd have a mutiny on his hands. But nothing could change Columbus' sense of destiny, nothing could erase the knowledge of God's inspired words that kept him on course. As he recorded in his journal on more than one occasion, the words of Scripture beckoned him onward:

> Listen to me, oh coastlands, and pay attention, you distant peoples. The Lord called me from the womb; from the body of my mother He named me...
>
> He said to me, "You are My servant, Israel, in whom I will display My glory... I will also make you a light for the nations, to bring My salvation to the ends of the Earth."[27]

And for the Puritans, who were being increasingly targeted by the Anglican Church in England, which relentlessly sought to destroy their growing movement, God's word shined a light of hope on their predicament that they couldn't help but apply to themselves.

> "Don't be afraid, because I'm with you; I'll bring your offspring from the east and gather you from the west. I'll say to the north: Give them up! And to the south: Don't hold them back! Bring My sons from afar, and My daughters from the ends of the Earth...
>
> "You are My witnesses," declares the Lord, "and My servant whom I have chosen, so that you may consider and believe Me and understand that I am He...
>
> "I am the Lord, your Holy One, the Creator of Israel, and your King." So says the Lord Who makes a way in the sea and a path through the surging waters...
>
> "Forget the former things; pay no attention to the things of old. Watch as I do something new; even now it's coming. Don't you see it? Indeed, I'll make a way in the wilderness and streams in the desert."[28]

What's more, the technological advances that occurred in Europe leading up to the discovery of America—particularly with Gutenberg's printing press in 1440—were such that all the forces occurring at the time would set the stage for all that followed. First came the Protestant Reformation, followed by the

---

27   Isaiah 49:1, 3, 6

28   Ibid. 43:5-6, 15-16, 18-19

Renaissance, which both occurred when many smaller European states were morphing into larger states, and all of them with a greater degree of centralized power.

More importantly, though, in the context of this work, that meant with the Reformation and Renaissance there came a greater sense of individualism just as a number of other societal forces came together to empower those individuals who previously could never hope to break free from centuries of collectivist, institutional control.

At the same time, nation-states like England, France, Spain, Portugal, and the Netherlands were suddenly able to take full advantage of several technological advances in shipbuilding, most notably with the caravel, a light sailing ship developed by the Portuguese in the late 1400s, which incorporated the use of a triangular sail, called a lateen, enabling ships to sail into the wind more effectively than any before in history. And that meant not only could a handful of European monarchs finance a series of ambitious oversea excursions, but a group of bold voyagers could also rise to new levels of exploration with the aid of navigational devices like the astrolabe, the quadrant, the magnetic compass, and the sextant, which in turn opened up new horizons of the sea.

It also meant that at just the right moment in history this newfound sense of individuality, which had been percolating for many centuries, would intersect with another personality trait so germane to biblical history, that of the outsider, as it pertains to the life of every chosen one of God. And that meant the world no longer consisted of a scattered, disarrayed band of outsiders but, rather, consisted of a whole generation of outsiders who were, all at once, ready to make their mark in the world—a world that was never the same again in the wake of their response to the call of God.

CHAPTER FOUR

UNIQUE AMONG NATIONS

*Then the Lord said to Abraham, "Leave your
country, your relatives, and your father's
household, and go to the land I will show you.
I'll make you into a great nation, and I'll bless
you; I'll make your name great so that you'll be a
blessing. I will bless those who bless you, and curse
those who curse you; and everyone on Earth will
be blessed through you." (Genesis 12:1-3)*

On What Basis

THERE ARE three myths about the creation of the United States of America that I hope to dispel throughout
the pages of this work. The first myth is that America
isn't special and so is wrong to think of itself as being unique
in the history of nations. The second myth is that it can only
be deemed legitimate if it was born in perfection—perfection
in morality, in liberty, and in equality. The third myth is that it
began in 1492, with the discovery of America by Christopher
Columbus, or in 1620, with the landing at Plymouth Rock by
the Pilgrims, or in 1776, with the signing of the Declaration of
Independence by the Founding Fathers.

As for the first myth, which I suggest is intertwined with
the second myth, I'd ask: "On what grounds do you insist that
America isn't special just because it wasn't perfect from birth?
Since when has any nation been deemed special on the basis

of its origins? Can this be said about the empires of antiquity like Egypt, Greece, or Rome? How about modern nations like France, Spain, or England?"

To which critics of America would quickly agree: "You're right to say America is no different from any other nation. So you admit it's not special or unique, is that it?"

"Not so fast," I'd reply just as quickly. "You don't think you can have it both ways, do you? On one hand, if you say America's claim of uniqueness is illegitimate because it wasn't conceived in perfection, then you're admitting to the possibility it could be special, if only it didn't fail to live up to its own expectations at various times in its history. And on the other hand, if you say it's no different from any other nation in history, then you have to withdraw your claim that it's illegitimate on the grounds it wasn't born in perfection. So, which is it?"

Conceived in Self-Determination

TRUTH IS, the United States of America is unique among nations because no other nation in history has come into being in the same way and under the same circumstances as it did. No other nation can point to a self-conscious moment in its history where it said: See, this is when we as a people chose a new way of life, a new form of government, conceived in self-determination, and aspiring to liberty and justice for all.

Yet ironically, it's this very aspect of America's origins that exposes it to intense criticism concerning its self-avowed aspirations, to morality, equality, and liberty. Because we aspire to worship, to speak, to live as we choose, any failure to live up to such high ideals plays directly into the hands of those who seek to undermine those aspirations. In other words, we're damned if we do, and damned if we don't.

What's more, although America is exposed to such criticism because of its commitment to these values, it's only vulnerable to such attacks as long as it remains ignorant of its true origins.

This brings us, then, to the third myth about America, which is that as much as we know about America's history in regard to Columbus, the Pilgrims, and the Founding Fathers, there's another aspect to its history that's generally unknown, if not downright suppressed. More ironic still, none of those who helped to establish America were even aware of this unknown aspect at the time, even as they faithfully performed their various roles on the stage of world history.

In short, while Columbus, the Pilgrims, and the Founding Fathers clearly identified with the plight of the heroes of their favorite book—*The Bible*—they weren't the only ones involved in establishing what we now know as America. That's because the creation of the United States of America didn't really begin in 1492, or 1620, or 1776, although one may rightly point to all of those dates as marking pivotal years in its creation.

Yes, it is true: When Scripture spoke of the wandering Israelites searching for a new homeland, Columbus wandered with them, searched with them, in his heart and mind. When Scripture spoke of God urging His chosen of Israel to repent of their wicked ways and reach out to Him in faith, the Pilgrims urged their countrymen to do for the Lord what those Israelites had failed to do. And when Scripture spoke of that band of Hebrew wanderers and outcasts who fell short of God's call, the Founding Fathers, too, hoped they'd one day comprise a band of wanderers and outcasts who did rise to the occasion.

However, while all these people may have identified with the Children of Israel, none of them for a moment would've dared believe there was any other connection between them and those with whom they identified. In other words, while those brave adventurers who forged a New World could identify with the Children of Israel, they knew they were as far removed from them as those who worship the stars of the silver screen are from the stars themselves. In the end, then, no amount of yearning to be a true son or daughter of Israel could ever make it so, no matter how hard one imagined oneself to be so.

Be that as it may, though, while this worldview pretty much represents the status quo as it's taught by way of mainstream historical analysis, there is actually another worldview concerning America's origins that completely rewrites the notion that its origins can be traced to 1492, 1620, or 1776.

It is to just such a new worldview that I'd like to speak to you now, a worldview that isn't really so new after all, historically speaking. Actually, much of the evidence that connects the creation of America beyond its assumed origins is something that began to come to light in the mid-1800s, with the birth of the marvelous science of archeology. And then only after much analysis of the archeological evidence, in concert with a new approach to the historical, scientific, and philological evidence, did the truth finally come to light.

It is to this very evidence, then, that this work will repeatedly turn to, in an earnest attempt to tell the real story of the promise of America, technology, and the New Earth.

One View Against Another

THE PRIMARY objection one encounters when discussing a subject like this is that most people find it hard to accept that God would act on behalf of any worldly nation, let alone act on behalf of one like America.

"What could be so special about any nation," they argue, "that would warrant God's unique blessing, ever since those golden days spoken of so reverently in Holy Scripture? That was then, and this is now. End of story."

To which I'd begin by pointing out something that all Christians claim to know but are somehow in denial over simply because of the power of human tradition. I'm talking about the clear declaration of Scripture that insists God is the same yesterday, today, and forever. If that's true, then how could anyone believe that God, once so involved with the Children of Israel, would suddenly check out of human history, never to be seen or heard from again?

Of course, having said that, we do have to admit that, on the surface, it does seem as though God has taken a vacation in regard to the history of nations. And if that's true, then how do we account for this apparent absence of God from the affairs of state?

Most certainly it's because of that much-misunderstood aspect of the divine nature we've already touched on, which is how God sometimes reveals Himself as an omnipotent, mysterious God, and other times as One Who is willing to localize His presence. In one place, Scripture has God declaring that He's the Alpha and the Omega, while in another, God declares that He's the God of Abraham, Isaac, and Jacob. As such, He's not just the God of the Universe, but He's also the God of a chosen few. In this willingness to localize Himself, He says to those who receive Him: "Here I am; here's My word. I'm not just omnipotent and mysterious, but I am also right here, right now, present with you, speaking with you, revealing Myself to you."

That's why Jesus had to tell His disciples, "You believe in God. Believe also in Me."[29] This from the One Whom these men saw walk on water, cause the blind to see and the deaf to hear; that calmed the storm and raised Lazarus from the dead with but a word. Yet this Man still felt He needed to remind them to not just believe in God above but also to believe in the One Who was standing in their midst. Why?

Jesus did so because He knew how hard it was for His disciples—and us—to equate the God of mystery and omnipotence with a God Who is willing to talk and commune with mere human beings. More than anything else, this dual nature of God, which both hides His reality and reveals it, lies at the heart of humanity's questions concerning the interaction between the supremely Divine and the merely human.

This duality of God explains why the atheist can never locate God, no matter how much he or she searches the Scriptures; and it explains why even a child can hear the voice of God in the whispering wind or a babbling brook. So, whether it's through the inspired pen of the writer of Holy Writ or the hidden hand of God in the world around us, this "localization of God," if I may call it that, has the potential to provide earthly access to an otherworldly God.

That said, I believe this dual aspect of God's revelatory nature lies at the heart of another dilemma. This one, however, doesn't concern the difference between atheists and believers, between an unseen God and a seen God; it's about how believers in one age of history are pitted against believers in another age, and how one historical view of the Divine is pitted against another view. What do I mean by that? Let me explain.

Having established God's willingness to localize His pres-

---

29   *John 14:1*

ence, we need to consider how this tendency relates to our experience in the here and now. We need to ask: How does this localization of God throughout time and space inform our understanding of the history of nations? How do the Scriptures themselves help us understand the way this localization process has unfolded from age to age? And how do we reconcile the idea of an infinite God with that of a finite volume of His revelation, comprising just sixty-six books of *The Bible*?

Questions like these are critical because when we moderns think about *The Bible* that we're so invested in, we neglect the fact that while we insist we're reading a book inspired by the God of eternity, we're actually clinging to a parochial version of that God because of the biblical translation we most revere. In short, though we claim to honor the eternal message of an eternal God, our real position focuses on a merely temporal slice of that message, however much we insist that it's a message *from* eternity *toward* eternity.

To demonstrate this, we turn to the book that best describes this dilemma we humans face when trying to grasp the eternal nature of God's word, as the mere mortals that we all are.

An Emerging Pattern

IN MANY WAYS, *The Bible* itself is a metaphor for this divine duality: Just as God both hides and reveals Himself, the message in Scripture reflects this same hiding and revealing—in its various translations throughout the ages—even as it tells the story of those to whom God is hiding and revealing Himself.

In fact, the central drama of *The Bible* is that of an infinite God Who repeatedly stoops down to interact with finite humans, how those humans respond in awe and reverence with this divine interaction, and how that marvelous relationship is inevitably spoiled by our presumption, pride, and selfishness.

It happened in the case of Adam and Eve, when God promised them eternal life, but they chose death. It happened in the case of Noah and his children after the Great Flood, when God promised to renew the Earth, but they gathered around a tower in rebellion. And it happened to the sons of Jacob, when God called them to be a blessing to the whole world, but jealousy drove them to sell their own brother Joseph into slavery. It happened when Moses led the Children of Israel out of Egyptian bondage, but the people preferred to worship a golden calf. It happened when Joshua led the Israelites in their occupation of the Promised Land, but they chose to serve the idols of the very people they were ordered to displace. It happened when a mighty nation was forged by the hand of David and Solomon, but was later divided, just like the heart of their king who loved many strange women. And it happened when Ezra and Nehemiah inspired the Jews to rebuild the Temple at Jerusalem after their return from Babylonian Captivity, but they embraced doubt and fear when their hope in that new day faded too soon.

Considering the purpose of *The Bible* is to reveal God's ways, you'd think that anyone reading it through the ages would pick up on this pattern and resist repeating this same tendency. But sadly, mere mortals that we are, we don't. As it is written:

> There came a man who was sent from God. His name was John. He came as a witness to testify about the Light so that through him everyone might believe. He himself wasn't the Light, but he came to testify about the Light.
>
> The true Light Who gives light to every man was coming into the world. He was in the world, and though the world was made through Him, the world didn't recognize Him. He came to His own, and His own received Him not.[30]

In all of this we see an emerging pattern—from Adam to Noah, from Jacob's sons to the Children of Israel, from the Jews in Ezra's day to those in Jesus' day. Again and again, we see an eternal God willingly commune with His mortal ones who then can't help but turn that willingness to localize His presence into something altogether alien from God's original plan.

God's Ultimate Plan

ADMITTEDLY, I'm compressing a great deal of history here to make my initial point, which I'll expand in subsequent chapters.

---

30 John 1:6-11

But hopefully, in doing so, my point won't go unappreciated. Because it's this dynamic between God's willingness to interact with humanity and our all-too-human response to that willingness that provides the bedrock of all that follows in this work.

Of course, many biblical historians—and just as many Christians—might argue that what I've just described is nothing new. I'm just repeating a familiar history; as Christians, we have to accept this, as if, as they say, "That is that," and there's nothing we can do to change it until the Lord returns someday. Yes, Jesus was crucified without accomplishing anything as earth-shattering as what those apocalyptic prophecies foresaw. But one day, history will see that future day, when God finally proves He's in control. No doubt the so-called "Church Age" has been an embarrassing period—punctuated as it's been by Dark Ages, Black Plagues, less-than-Holy Crusades, Inquisitions, Star Chambers, witch hunts, and sundry religious wars in which the brethren wantonly murdered one another in the name of God, etc., etc., etc.

But what can you really expect, right? I mean, based on what I've already described, as our perennial tendency toward presumption, pride, and selfishness, what more would we expect after God checked out some two thousand years ago? Sure, Jesus came, sure, Jesus died and resurrected, and then He certainly did leave. What are we to do, then? Certainly, we have no choice but to hope for the best, and keep a stiff upper lip until Jesus returns in all His glory.

And can you really blame us for feeling this way? I mean, isn't that pretty much how the traditional view of biblical history portrays our lot in life? The only hope for the true believer is to die and go to Heaven, or to get raptured out of the present mess, or for the Lord to finally split the sky, like He's promised, and save us like the cavalry coming to the rescue.

But is that really all there is to God's control over history?

Let's review: So God created the Earth in seven days, along with every living creature on it; He commanded Adam and Eve and their descendants to overspread the planet; He restarted the whole process with Noah and his family after the Flood; then He upped the ante with Abraham and his sons.

Then the Lord said to Abraham, "Leave your country, your relatives, and your father's household, and go to the land I will show you.

"I'll make you into a great nation, and I'll bless you; I'll make your name great, so that you'll be a blessing.

"I will bless those who bless you, and curse those who curse you; and everyone on Earth will be blessed through you."[31]

Then, when Paul of Tarsus was knocked off his horse, and he "saw the Light," he saw that Jesus Christ was the vehicle through which God was manifesting that very first promise to Abraham. As Paul later described it in his letter to the Galatians:

The Scriptures foresaw that God would justify the Gentiles by faith, and foretold the gospel to Abraham: "All nations will be blessed through you."[32]

So, God did all that, but then ever since—according to most Christian traditions—He's just been looking down upon the affairs of humanity, high above it all, for more than two thousand years now. Like a dispassionate cheerleader, God has been rooting for the saints, as they slug it out with the devil and his minions, ever since Jesus gave it His best shot on Calvary, and then vacated the scene, headed for greener pastures in Heaven. He did, after all, tell Pontius Pilate, that His Kingdom was not of this world, did He not? Christians, ever since, have been singing, "This world is not my home; I'm just a-passing through." So again, "That," as they say, "is that." Right?

But wait. Haven't I myself already confirmed this view of biblical history, regarding the emerging pattern I described earlier? Well, yes, I do confess I did. But fortunately, for our sakes, God knows all-too-well about this pattern, and so He's built into His word not just a description of this tendency but also an antidote for it, if only we'll pay attention to the clues. Because tucked away in the biblical storyline, from Adam to Christ, there are numerous promises of God—as we'll soon begin to see—

31　Genesis 12:1-3

32　Galatians 3:8

which are more than capable of counteracting any human failures that might threaten God's ultimate plan for humanity.

Every Stream of History

NOW AT THIS point we'd do well to remember something very important about the promises of God in *The Bible*. When it comes to understanding the true nature of these promises, many of them are conditional and require a response from the recipients before God keeps those promises, while many are unconditional, regardless of whether the recipients cooperate in their fulfillment. Make the mistake of overlooking this critical aspect of biblical interpretation, and you run the risk of never being able to answer the question of whether God is keeping any of the promises found in Scripture.

A perfect example of the difference between conditional and unconditional promises of God can be seen in, naturally enough, the first book of *The Bible*:

> And the Lord commanded Adam, "You may eat freely from every tree of the garden, but you must not eat from the Tree of the Knowledge of Good and Evil, because the day you do, you will certainly die."[33]

Now in the case of this first conditional promise to Adam, admittedly, it was a promise in reverse. By that I mean it wasn't a promise of what Adam could look forward to if he obeyed God. Still, it was such that, if Adam had obeyed God's command, then God would have certainly kept His end of the bargain by sustaining Adam's life indefinitely.

In contrast, an example of an unconditional promise quickly followed on the heels of this tragic event; and something also to keep in mind is this pattern of when God's people fail to meet the demands of a conditional promise, the next promise God utters is usually an unconditional one. In this case, although God is apparently speaking to the serpent, He's really speaking to the devil for his role in mankind's downfall, and thus to us by way of that conversation.

---

33 *Genesis 2:16-17*

So the Lord said to the serpent, "Because you've done this thing … I'll create division between you and the woman, between your children and her children. He'll crush your head, and you'll bruise his heel."[34]

In this primordial promise, God predicts something that is neither dependent upon Adam or Eve's cooperation nor upon any of the children that God speaks of here. In fact, the fulfillment of this promise, which speaks of the Advent of Christ, is such that every stream of history will yield to the performance of this promise, come Hell or high water.

It is to just such promises, then, which are unconditional in nature, that we'll concern ourselves in the pages that follow—promises like the one we just saw concerning God's word to Abraham:

Leave your country… Go to the land I'll show you… I'll make you into a great nation… I'll make your name great … and everyone on Earth will be blessed through you.[35]

That said, it's time now to bring together all the building blocks to establish a firm foundation for this work.

The Antidote

SO FAR we've pointed to how an omnipotent, mysterious God has willingly localized His presence in the midst of His creation, and our human tendency to take that eternal message and focus on a merely temporal slice of that message. Without going into too much detail yet, we posed questions like: How does this localization of God throughout time and space inform our current understanding of the history of nations? How do the Scriptures themselves help us understand the way this localization process has unfolded from age to age? And how do we reconcile the idea of an infinite God with that of a finite volume of His revelation, comprising just sixty-six books of *The Bible*?

Again, without going into too much detail yet, in our initial

---

34   Genesis 3:14-15

35   Ibid. 12:1-3

look of this localization process, we pointed out how a pattern emerged, from the days of Adam to Jesus. Although God created the world and everyone in it, the world still finds it incredibly difficult to recognize Him: He comes to His own, He reveals Himself to His own, but, by and large, His own receive Him not.

And finally, even when Jesus fulfilled the ultimate promise of God to humanity, with His life, death, and resurrection, we saw how most Christian traditions viewed our ability to short-circuit such efforts as inevitable. Even in the wake of Christ's inauguration of a great new era, with the birth of the so-called "Church Age," humans still couldn't help but undermine that effort, too, with their various Inquisitions, Star Chambers, witch hunts, and religious wars.

At that point I insisted God's word still contained an antidote for this human tendency, something that I believe is embedded there for anyone who is willing to pay attention to the clues. That "something" I then suggested—the antidote—is found in the form of the promises of God, and more specifically, those promises of God that are unconditional in nature, as opposed to those that are conditional.

These various ingredients, then, will blend together to provide answers to questions like: How does an omnipotent, mysterious God intend to overcome our tendency to foul up His plan for humanity? If God anticipated this human tendency and uttered promises uniquely geared to address this issue, how can we re-evaluate the last two thousand plus years of world history in light of this possibility? And more importantly, which promises of God should we pay attention to, even while Christians today insist that they no longer apply to modern nations like America and her various counterparts throughout the world?

CHAPTER FIVE

THE KINGDOM OF STONE

*In the days of those kings, the God of Heaven
will set up a kingdom that will never be
destroyed, nor will it be left to another people.
It will shatter all these kingdoms and bring
them to an end, but will itself stand forever.
And just as you saw a stone being cut out of
the mountain without human hands, and it
shattered the iron, clay, bronze, silver, and
gold, so the great God has told the king what
will happen in the future. (Daniel 2:44)*

The Hope of Israel

LONG BEFORE the Pilgrims wrestled with the question of how to further establish the Kingdom of God on Earth, and long after the Children of Israel wrestled with the same thing, another group of outsiders wrestled with it, too. All their lives, the disciples of Jesus had heard about what the prophets of old predicted: By way of Israel's descendants, the whole world would one day be blessed, and through them, all would finally come to a knowledge of the one, true God.

Yet flying in the face of such a glorious destiny were centuries of failure, tragedy, and hopelessness. Despite all the valiant efforts of the sons and daughters of Jacob, the hope of Israel always seemed just out of reach. For the disciples, as proud men, and for Israel, as a once-mighty nation, the fire that had burned so brightly slowly faded until it was nothing more than a smoldering ember threatening to go out at any moment.

Fortunately for them—and for the world—the repeated failures of national Israel didn't spell the end of God's plan to bless all mankind. Despite every misstep on the part of humanity—and every attempt of Satan to derail this salvation plan—God always had a failsafe maneuver to right the ship if it ever veered off course. At some point in human history, something—or rather Someone—was scheduled to bridge the gap, in making God's plan for mankind a reality in spite of all our repeated failures. According to prophecy, this Someone would arrive one day when all hope was lost—the Day of the Lord, it was called—the day when all wrongs would be made right, when the shame of downtrodden Israel would be removed and her rightful place as head of the nations would be established.

So when word spread throughout the countryside, of the Man Jesus Who healed the sick and gave sight to the blind, the dying embers of the old dream began to rekindle. Before long, this Jesus had gathered about Himself a group of eager young men who were all anxious to know more about the hope of Israel. What is it really? Is it a place? Is it a state of mind? Are You the One, Jesus, Who we've waited for all this time? Are You the One Who will finally restore this hope of ours, to establish the Kingdom of God, once and for all?

Words in Secret

NO DOUBT the most famous prayer of all time is the one that Jesus taught His disciples to pray. After becoming more and more convinced of the truth that this amazing Man was telling them, those closest to Him wanted to know more. After all, this was the Man Whom they saw give sight to the blind and hearing to the deaf, that healed the sick and cast out demons with but a word. Certainly, if anyone knew what God was really like it was this Man, so they asked Him, "Lord, teach us to pray."[36] So He did, and ever since, we've been the beneficiaries of that insight-

---

36 *Luke 11:1*

ful prayer. Yet to those who take the time to thoroughly consider this scene in *The Bible*, one can't help but be struck by several, dare I say, inconsistencies.

Now before anyone assumes that by inconsistencies I mean to say there are inconsistencies with the prayer itself, let me be clear; this isn't at all what I'm suggesting. No, the inconsistencies I'm talking about have nothing to do with the prayer of Jesus but, rather, with humanity's beliefs about this prayer. Because in reality, while this prayer should rightly be considered one of the great benchmarks in Christian theology, it's only upon further review of this scene that we come face to face with how far we've fallen short of the mark in truly appreciating what's communicated in this simple yet potent prayer.

To demonstrate what I mean by this, let's first consider its well-known title. Now anyone who knows about the original biblical manuscripts knows there were no chapter or verse designations in Scripture, which means there were no chapter or verse headings, either, and thus there was never a title to this prayer. In its original form, the gospel narrative simply records that the disciples asked Jesus to teach them to pray, and so He did. In fact, the most obvious clue that this scene contains inconsistencies is that it should never have been called the Lord's Prayer in the first place. Why?

Well, of course, that's because Jesus Himself never prayed this prayer. He never prayed, "Father, forgive Me of My sins, even as I forgive others of their sins." If you want to find the true Lord's prayer in *The Bible*, you need to look at the seventeenth chapter of *The Gospel of John*, where Jesus prayed concerning His imminent departure and what was to become of His disciples in the aftermath of His death. "Father," prayed Jesus, "please make all of us one in the Spirit, even as You and I are one."[37]

Of course many might argue that it makes no difference what we call the prayer; all one needs to do is consider its contents. Others might argue that I'm splitting hairs by pointing this out. But I assure you I'm only doing this to get the ball rolling, to demonstrate just how powerful tradition is and how it invariably

---

37   John 17:21

becomes a barrier to knowledge instead of what Jesus intends it to be, which is a gateway.

We see evidence of this when the disciples asked Jesus to teach them to pray. Consider what He told them before He taught them this prayer. Anyone who has ever read *The Bible* has read the words. But how many have ever stopped to ask: Before praying this most sacred prayer, am I obeying Christ's introductory remarks to this prayer?

Now, mind you, we're talking about a prayer that countless Christians have prayed down through the ages ever since that day Jesus taught it to His disciples. Yet ironically, although we've often heard this warning, even as the ministers of God lead us in this prayer, the words go unheeded. What is this introduction to—what has rightly been suggested that we call—the Disciples' Prayer?

> So Jesus told His disciples, "And when you pray, don't be like the hypocrites, because they love to pray in the synagogues and on street corners to be seen by others. Truly I tell you, they've received their reward in full. But when you pray, go into your room, close the door and pray to your Father Who is unseen. Then your Father, Who sees what's done in secret, will reward you.
>
> "And when you pray, avoid vain repetitions like the pagans who think they'll be heard because of their many words. Don't be like them, because your Father knows what you need before you ask Him. This, then, is how you should pray: 'Our Father Who is in Heaven, holy is Your name. Your Kingdom come, Your will be done, on Earth as it is in Heaven...'"[38]

So I ask you: If Jesus introduced this prayer, by telling us what to avoid when we pray to God, wouldn't we want to honor Him in His simple yet straightforward request? Of course we would. But *have* we honored that request? When we pray this prayer, do we first go into our room, close the door, and pray these words in secret? When we pray this prayer, do we avoid repeating it, word-for-word, time after time, year in and year

---

38 *Matthew 6:5-9*

out, because we assume God will bless us just because we voiced this special prayer?

So much for actually paying attention to the request of Jesus. So much for thinking we realize what we're doing when we fall in line by publicly repeating this prayer over and over again.

Now, in pointing out such inconsistencies in regard to this special prayer, my purpose is not to condemn anyone for following along in the traditional manner of praying this prayer. If it were my goal to condemn anyone for following the dictates of their conscience, I assure you this work would never have been produced for your consideration. Instead, my point in insisting that we honestly address such inconsistencies is done simply for the sake of all that follows here.

In short, I hope that as we re-examine the meaning, purpose, and implications of this special prayer, you keep in mind the preceding inconsistencies. If you feel that I'm contradicting what you know or have been taught about this prayer, first ask yourself if it might not be another inconsistency so characteristic of a traditional view of Scripture, as opposed to what it might really be saying. Before you reject what I'm proposing, please consider that just as countless saints have been misled about praying the so-called "Lord's Prayer," in public and *ad nauseam*, there might be other aspects of this prayer that are just as misunderstood and overlooked.

The Deepest Truths of Scripture

IT HAS rightly been observed that the deepest truths of *The Bible* are paradoxical in nature. Ignore this central fact and one is sure to misunderstand everything written in it. Just as importantly, it's critical to take note of the enormous difference between inconsistencies and paradoxes.

Inconsistencies, as in the case of the previous scene involving the "Lord's Prayer," don't occur because of any contradictions in God's word itself but, rather, because of human ignorance stemming from a blind adherence to traditions about it.

Paradoxes, on the other hand, stem from the fact that divine truth is not something humans are meant to grasp at first glance. Due to the paradoxical nature of God, the truth of Scripture is something we must wrestle with, live with, struggle with, before we begin to embrace what is always hidden in plain sight.

As defined in the dictionary, a paradox is "an apparently contradictory statement that, when investigated or explained, may actually prove to be true." Notice that in the case of a paradox, what's initially viewed as a contradiction is nevertheless negated when it's sufficiently investigated.

As a matter of fact, *The Bible* is full of apparent contradictions that are usually ignored or go unnoticed, but which, when pointed out, trigger all manner of frustration in the believer, not to mention great delight in the skeptic.

For example, at one point in Scripture, Christ is referred to as the Prince of Peace,[39] yet elsewhere Jesus declared that He didn't come to bring peace but to bring a sword.[40] That's a contradiction, right? No, it's a paradox.

In fact, when it comes to paradoxes in *The Bible*, there's no greater example of this than the teachings of Jesus Himself. In one place, He says, "Seek and you'll find,"[41] while elsewhere He says, "Whoever seeks to save their life will lose it, but whoever loses their life for My sake will save it."[42] A contradiction? No, a paradox.

Again, Jesus told His disciples, "Look, I'm sending you out like sheep amongst wolves; therefore, be harmless as doves but wise as serpents."[43] Doves are cute and cuddly; serpents hiss and bite. Yet Jesus expected His disciples—no, He commanded them—to be one and the same, as if He expected them to embrace two natures in a single body. That's a contradiction, right? No… You've got it now; it's a paradox.

In fact, Jesus didn't just teach the deepest truths of Scripture by way of paradox; He was Himself a walking, talking paradox.

For Greek philosophers, like Plato and Aristotle, a paradox is impossible. According to them, two different things can never be the same thing. Such logic states: "*If* this, *then* that." Conse-

---

39   Isaiah 9:6

40   Matthew 10:34

41   Ibid. 7:7

42   Luke 9:24; 17:33

43   Matthew 10:16

quently, if the Greek gods were immortal, then they were qualitatively distinct from humans, because humans die. Therefore, *if a god, then* not human.

This kind of logic, however, was turned inside out in the life and death of Jesus, Who though proving Himself to be God in the flesh was still capable of suffering death. Although not Aristotelians themselves, the Jews of Jesus' day exhibited this same sort of logical frame of reference in their reaction to the claims of Jesus. The fact that He was clearly human made it impossible for most of them to accept that He was the Christ. At the same time, His insistence that, as the Son of Man, He was destined to die was also impossible for them to conceive because, to them, the Son of Man was a messianic figure of godlike proportions Who was therefore impervious to death.

Yet, in complete defiance of such logic, Jesus was, according to Scripture, both God and Man in a single Person. He was capable of all that God was capable of, as demonstrated by His power to perform miracles at will, yet capable of all that Man was capable of, as demonstrated by His humiliation, suffering, and death.

That said, let's see how this awareness of the difference between inconsistencies and paradoxes provides us with a new view of what I believe should be called the Disciples' Prayer.

Hanging in the Balance

FIRST TRY to imagine what the disciples were thinking when they asked Jesus to teach them to pray.

As Jews living through decades of Roman domination, these men, like generations before them, were anticipating divine deliverance at the hands of a messianic figure. According to prophecies in such works as *The First Book of Enoch*, an all-powerful figure—the Son of Man, as Enoch called Him—was supposed to topple whatever government existed at the time of His arrival and restore the nation of Israel as the dominating force in world history.

The prophet Daniel also spoke of this Son of Man Who would be given "dominion, glory, and kingship, that the people of every nation and language should serve Him. His dominion is an everlasting dominion that won't pass away, and His Kingdom is one that will never be destroyed."[44] As biblical scholars will all tell you, the Roman Empire wasn't the only kingdom to oppress the nation of the Jews. According to Daniel, four great empires were to dominate the southern kingdom of Judah. We know this because the king of the first empire had a disturbing dream, which Daniel alone, among all the wise men of Babylon, was able to interpret. Said Daniel to King Nebuchadnezzar:

> As you were watching, oh king, a great statue appeared. A great and dazzling statue stood before you, and its form was awesome. The head of the statue was pure gold, its chest and arms were silver, its belly and thighs were bronze, its legs were iron, and its feet were part iron and part clay.
>
> As you watched, a stone was cut out of a mountain, but not by human hands. It struck the statue on its feet of iron and clay, and crushed them. Then the iron, clay, bronze, silver, and gold were shattered and became like chaff on the threshing floor in summer. The wind carried them away, and not a trace of them could be found. But the stone that had struck the statue became a great mountain and filled the whole Earth.[45]

Daniel went on to explain the meaning of the king's dream, saying this great statue represented four empires, of which Babylon was the head of gold, and which would be followed by three more empires. These kingdoms, say biblical scholars, quite unanimously, are revealed later in *The Book of Daniel* to be Medo-Persia, Greece, and Rome.[46] But what scholars are not so unanimous about is the identity of the Kingdom of Stone. Said Daniel:

> In the days of those kings, the God of Heaven will set up a kingdom that will never be destroyed, nor will it be left to another people. It will shatter all these kingdoms and

---

44   *Daniel 7:14*

45   *Ibid. 2:31-35*

46   *Ibid. 7*

bring them to an end, but will itself stand forever. And just as you saw a stone being cut out of the mountain without human hands, and it shattered the iron, clay, bronze, silver, and gold, so the great God has told the king what will happen in the future.[47]

One of the great mysteries of biblical prophecy, this Stone Kingdom is rarely if ever spoken of in any sermon or commentary. More often than not, though, if the subject is broached, we're told that this kingdom represents the Second Coming of Christ. The only problem with that interpretation is, this is only possible if you twist Daniel's method of interpretation. Clearly, Daniel intended his listeners to understand that the imagery of Nebuchadnezzar's dream of the Great Image represents earthly kingdoms. Nothing at all indicates that the symbolism contained in the dream has shifted, or else why not simply do what Daniel did seven chapters later in his description of four beasts that also represent Babylon, Medo-Persia, Greece, and Rome? There, when Jesus arrived on the scene of biblical prophecy, Daniel plainly stated that One like the Son of Man took His place on the stage of world history.

Of course none of this is new when it comes to the foibles of interpreting biblical prophecy. Due to the ambiguous nature of the symbolism contained in Scripture, one is always faced with the question of how to approach what God means to reveal. Here again we come face to face with the paradoxical nature of God's word. And again this ambiguity, which spawns all kinds of inconsistencies in interpretation, is something that critics and skeptics of *The Bible* love to pounce on, in their insistence that nothing in Scripture can be depended on to reveal truth.

But if God exists and He's revealed His truth in Scripture, then don't you think He's aware of the ambiguous nature of that message? Of course He is; so evidently this is how God has purposely designed it. Had He chosen to be more specific, then certainly He'd have spelled out His message as plainly as the nose on your face. But in couching His word in such symbolism, it inevitably forces us to search long and hard for its true

---

47 Daniel 2:44

meaning. Clearly King Solomon had this in mind when he said, "It's the glory of God to conceal a matter and the honor of kings to search it out."[48] Add to that the extent to which we humans naturally see inconsistencies instead of seeking to resolve the paradox of God's word, and we can only assume the disciples of Jesus fell victim to this same tendency.

Imagine what the disciples were thinking, then, when they asked Jesus to teach them to pray. Brutally oppressed by their Roman overlords, the disciples were anxious for Jesus to tell them something that would give them hope in a world where all hope seemed lost: "Lord, when will the glorious promises of our God finally deliver us from oppression and set us free? How much longer, Jesus, will You wander about as a mere itinerant preacher while we wait so patiently? And with our lives hanging in the balance every moment, what is taking You so long to manifest Your power?"

So there the disciples were, waiting and wondering, when Jesus—Whom they were increasingly coming to believe was their long-awaited Messiah—would say the word and smash the Roman Empire into oblivion. Firmly believing this Man Who healed the sick and tamed the wind could accomplish such an impossibility, the disciples expected Jesus to call them to action at any moment. With yet another command from His lips, the Roman Empire would collapse around them, and the Stone Kingdom they'd heard about their whole lives would finally inaugurate a new era of peace and tranquility upon the Earth.

Keep in mind that, in hindsight, we know what the disciples could have never known at the time when they asked Him to teach them to pray. Looking back, we know Jesus chose to not overthrow the Roman Empire in the way the Jews in that day expected the Messiah to do. All too often we in the present are faced with the near impossible task of ridding ourselves of this hindsight. But unless we do, we'll never be able to truly understand the disciples' reaction to the prayer Jesus uttered that day.

This is doubly important when we remember that when the disciples were called to follow Jesus, they weren't yet the saintly creatures we think of. These were still earthy, hard-fisted men,

---

48 *Proverbs 25:2*

not scholars, not holy men. They were fishermen, tax collectors, and the like, men who had yet to be humbled and molded by the hand of the Master, as can be seen when John and James asked to one day be seated beside Jesus in His heavenly Kingdom. But He rebuked them for requesting positions of such eminence and authority. Instead, they were to follow His example:

> Just as the Son of Man didn't come to be served but to serve, and to give His life as a ransom for many, you must realize that to be first in the Kingdom of Heaven, you should seek to be last. And anyone who wants to be a master must become a slave to all.[49]

Now tell me: When the disciples heard this, do you think they openly embraced so paradoxical a lesson? Or did they instead balk at what they could only see at the time as a total inconsistency?

Undoubtedly, what the disciples were really thinking when they asked Jesus to teach them to pray was: Now that we know Who You are and what You're capable of, Jesus, what should we do while we patiently wait for You to manifest Your Kingdom of Stone? We see You praying to God above, and as a result, great miracles are wrought by Your hand. So please, as You prepare to crush the kingdoms of the Earth with Your mighty power, can You teach us to pray so we can partake of the miracles You perform among men?

But in response to their veiled request, to learn how to pray, Jesus replied:

> So, then, this is how you should pray: "Our Father Who is in Heaven, holy is Your name. Your Kingdom come, Your will be done, on Earth as it is in Heaven."[50]

Okay, so far, so good, they might have thought. God's will is going to be done here on Earth, presumably done through our hands, just as we see it being done through the hands of Jesus.

But then, rather than keep the ball rolling, rather than invoke more of Heaven's mighty power in their midst, Jesus took

---

49   *Mark 10:43-45*

50   *Matthew 6:9-10*

a distinctively mundane turn away from their heavenly aspirations. Jesus continued:

> "And give us this day our daily bread, and forgive us our sins, as we forgive those who sin against us. And lead us not into temptation, but deliver us from evil."[51]

Wait, what? Daily bread? Sins? Temptation? Well, okay, Lord, if You say so.

One can only imagine the disappointment that the disciples might have felt. Here they were hoping for something that could have helped them in their hour of need, something to lift them out of their downtrodden condition. But instead, Jesus offered them not power and dominion but bread and forgiveness.

And just in case you think I'm exaggerating, notice, if you will, that even future generations have garnished this prayer to make it sound better. While Jesus was perfectly content to end His version of this prayer with the part about our praying that God deliver us from evil, at some point in time others in the Church felt a similar compunction to end this prayer with a little more pizzazz. Not content to simply end on Jesus' original note, now we, like the disciples of old, feel the need to invoke one last verse to clinch the deal. Ever since that minor yet all-important edit, we pray:

> "And lead us not into temptation, but deliver us from evil, for Yours is the Kingdom, and the power, and the glory, forevermore. Amen!"

Now, that's what I call an ending—a proper ending for a prayer straight from On-High.

But please, before anyone accuses me of being too harsh in my treatment of the disciples, or anyone among us who is just as prone to seek more from Heaven than what Jesus wants for us, I confess that I too am guilty of this same tendency. After all, "it takes one, to know one," right? So, in pointing out the inconsistencies of this scene, I repeat, it isn't my intention to condemn or ridicule anyone for their sincere beliefs. My only hope is to shed new light on this subject, which can only be gained from

---

51 *Matthew 6:11-13*

a willingness to revisit this familiar scene. And in courageous-ly re-examining ages-long traditions, I hope to further mine the depths of this special prayer, as God has intended it to be mined all along.

By enabling us to see this prayer in a new light, I also hope to lay the foundation for a new view to show that God is still in the business of guiding the nations of the world. More specifically, I'm speaking of the role of that enigmatic Kingdom of Stone described by Daniel. As we proceed, we'll be especially inter-ested in how this kingdom helps focus many of the inquiries we've introduced so far, such as: To what extent is God's habit of hiding and revealing Himself displayed not only in terms of ancient history but modern history as well? What clues are there to indicate God is still guiding nations and individuals to this day? And finally, how might these clues help us better under-stand God's plan for America, technology, and the New Earth, in the context of the divine response to our prayer for God's will to be done on Earth as it is in Heaven?

Chapter Six

MISTAKES OF THE PAST

May the Lord cause you to flourish, both you and your children. May you be blessed by the Lord, the Maker of Heaven and Earth. The Heavens belong to the Lord, but the Earth He has given to mankind. (Psalm 115:14-16)

Free Food and Miracles

AS IT WAS then, so it is now. The dilemma of the disciples in Jesus' day is really no different from ours today. As the disciples were concerned with maintaining their national identity and personal security, in a world bent on subduing them, we too struggle to maintain our identity and security in a world just as determined to subdue us. All too often, when our future is clouded in uncertainty, like the disciples of old, we're also tempted to seek more from God than what He desires for us. We seek shortcuts to personal happiness at the expense of eternal happiness; we seek to exchange personal security in the present tense in exchange for the eternal security that God promises us if only we do things His way. Too often we fail to understand what the Scriptures reveal, even though they were written specifically for our benefit.

Thus, the same choice is presented to us, just as it was presented to those who stood in the presence of Jesus. But will we notice what others fail to notice? Will we learn from the mistakes of the past, or are we doomed to repeat those same mistakes?

As long as Jesus was passing out free food and miracles, the crowds were so thick about Him that as He traveled from city to city He could hardly make His way through the mass of people. But no sooner did He begin to explain the cost of following Him than the crowds slowly began to thin. The more Jesus spoke of taking up one's cross, the less people clamored for His blessings. It's not as though the Lord was no longer willing to impart His blessings; but as soon as people were challenged to be more than recipients of God's blessings, they suddenly found themselves too busy to bother.

More than anyone else, then, Jesus understands the tendency of His creation to shirk the demands of a life truly devoted to God, to withhold what we as creatures of God must render to Him in this life. Like spoiled, undisciplined children, we want the goodies without delivering the goods. So when Jesus taught the disciples to pray, "Our Father Who is in Heaven, holy is Your name. Your Kingdom come, Your will be done, on Earth as it is in Heaven," what do you think went through their minds? Did they understand the implications of these words as they pertained to God's purpose for humanity? Or did they instead think of this prayer in terms of what they hoped God would do for them? Of course, I'd suggest, just like the rest of us, they tended to see how it spoke more to their desires than to God's.

To repeat: As it was then, so it is now. Ask yourself: When we consider how we view this prayer when we pray it, what are we really hoping for? Are we hoping to become genuine instruments that God will use to manifest His heavenly Kingdom here on Earth? Or are we really hoping to be whisked away someday to be where the God of Heaven is? In short, do we assume what most assume: The goal of the Christian has nothing to do with our earthly life down here and everything to do with our being deemed worthy to go to Heaven when we die? Ask a hundred Christians, and certainly ninety-nine of them would say it is.

This Manifest Destiny

BUT CONSIDERING our earlier discussion about the difficulty of reconciling paradoxes while others see only inconsistencies, I insist that we're wrestling with this same age-old dilemma. That's because there's actually far more scriptural evidence that suggests God's true goal for His saints has nothing to do with their dying and going to Heaven. Instead, what we see is that, when Jesus taught His disciples to pray, "Your will be done on Earth as it is in Heaven," He was just reminding us of what *The Bible* has been revealing to humanity since time immemorial:

> May the Lord cause you to flourish, both you and your children. May you be blessed by the Lord, the Maker of Heaven and Earth. The Heavens belong to the Lord, but the Earth He has given to mankind.[52]

In fact, when Jesus taught His disciples to pray that day, He was doing the same thing as when He reminded His listeners that "when you love others as you love yourself," you're obeying all of God's commandments rolled into one. Similarly, when we pray for "God's will to be done on Earth," we're encapsulating, in a deceptively simple prayer, everything God has commissioned us to do ever since our first parents were told to populate the whole Earth, since Noah and his family were told to go forth from the ark, and since the Children of Israel were told to inherit the land God had promised to Abraham.

Of Adam and Eve, it is written:

> So God created mankind in His own image; in the image of God He created them; male and female He created them. God blessed them, and said to them, "Be fruitful and multiply, and fill the Earth and subdue it."[53]

This idea was later echoed by the psalmist, when he said:

> What is mankind that You're mindful of them, human beings that You care for them? You've made them a little lower than God, and You crowned them with glory and majesty! You made them rulers over the works of Your hands; You've put everything under their feet.[54]

---

52   *Psalm 115:14-16*

53   *Genesis 1:27-28*

54   *Psalm 8:4-6*

So, from Adam and Eve, to Noah and the Children of Israel, God established a divine precedent—a precedent that has never been set aside, despite what traditions might say to the contrary. Clearly, there have been setbacks in every phase of this commission. Clearly, there have been endless mistakes in that faltering attempt. Yet at every stage of this grand migration, the people of God have managed to progress, slowly but surely, toward the goal of this divine march of the ages.

Naturally, the devil at every turn has inspired his minions to short-circuit the inexorable movement toward this manifest destiny. One famous example of this occurred after the Great Flood, when God reiterated this plan.

> Then God blessed Noah and his sons, saying to them, "Be fruitful and increase in number and fill the Earth."[55]

But what happened soon afterward? Nimrod, the grandson of Ham and great-grandson of Noah, sought to reverse this divine calling by uniting the people with a common language.

One of the most persistent misconceptions of *The Bible* is that in Nimrod's day everyone spoke a single language, which only changed after God struck at this unity with what is called the Confusion of Tongues. But this is dispelled when we read the previous chapter in *Genesis*, where we find that before the Tower of Babel, all the sons of Noah lived separately, and in their divided state, they all spoke the unique language of their family. As it is written, speaking first of the sons of Japheth:

> From these, the maritime peoples *spread out* into their territories by their clans within their nations, each with its own language... These are the sons of Ham by their clans and languages, in their territories and nations... These are the sons of Shem by their clans and languages, in their territories and nations... These are the clans of Noah's sons, according to their lines of descent, within their nations. From these, the nations *spread out* over the Earth after the Flood.[56]

---

55 *Genesis 9:1*

56 *Ibid. 10:5, 20, 31-32*

Not until the following chapter do we read how Nimrod united the people in a common language, thereby reversing this initial trend toward a diversity of languages which preceded the scattering that took place at the Tower of Babel. In the story of Nimrod and his tower, then, we see the first recorded attempt to thwart God's plan to have humanity fill the Earth after the Flood. As it turned out, Nimrod was only able to reverse this migration by homogenizing the language of the people; and because of Scripture's portrayal of this domination of Nimrod's language, later generations have simply assumed the whole world spoke the same language from the beginning.

This pattern in *The Bible*—of dividing, scattering, and uniting—is so important, in fact, that several points must be noted if we're to understand the story contained in this work. In relating the promise of America, technology, and the New Earth, we'll be looking at how these divinely ordained migrations play out through the long ages of history. And for those who care to look, God's word will provide the key to deciphering this drama. More specifically, we're talking about several words used throughout the scriptural record to describe this interplay between God's command to spread out and fill the Earth, and Satan's attempt to thwart this worldwide dispersion of peoples.

So when *The Bible* describes the clans of Noah, as "spreading out" into their own territories, we encounter a Hebrew word, *parad*, that reveals a great deal about what I'll be trying to demonstrate throughout this investigation. In addition to its meaning of spreading out, it also speaks of "dispersing," "dividing," "scattering," "separating," and "unfolding." Again and again, for those who care to notice, we'll see how words like *parad*, and several others like it, all speak of dividing, scattering, and separating, and which together will provide us with critical signposts to guide us throughout this divine drama.

In Defiance of God's Command

WITH THIS in mind, let's return to our scene of Noah, his sons, and their families after the Great Flood. In this we see something similar to the story of America. Just as America was once called the New World, the world after the receding flood waters in Noah's day can also be considered a new world. The human race had been given a new lease on life in the wake of a terrible abuse of power, which a traditional view of Scripture ignores. That's because an important biblical account was censored after several early Church Fathers deemed it too controversial for the masses. Without the background information provided by this "lost book" of *The Bible*, the real reason God destroyed the Earth would have eluded mankind for all time.

I'm referring to a book I mentioned earlier: *The First Book of Enoch*. In this ancient text, we find written evidence that God didn't flood the Earth just because humanity succumbed to the sins of the flesh, as though God was somehow shocked by human sin. This isn't meant to diminish the tragedy of sin but instead to point out that while sin has marred God's plan for humanity, it can never account for God unleashing the Flood. No, much more disturbing to God was what Enoch chronicled in his book concerning those angelic beings called the Watchers. It was they who necessitated the Great Flood. More specifically, it was their human offspring whom *Genesis* calls the *Nephilim*—the giants—who according to Enoch began to multiply and destroy all life on Earth. Were it not for the need to destroy that monstrous race of giants, the Flood would never have been required.

Now it may seem out of place to be telling a tale of giants when speaking of the promise of America, technology, and the New Earth. But I assure you that further down the road in this unfolding drama, we will return to the implications of this fantastic tale. In the meantime, however, barring certain Church Fathers' disapproval of such an incredible tale, suffice it to say, we're presently looking to this chapter of biblical history as a fitting parallel. Why do I say that?

I do so because to understand how the existence of America fits into the entire biblical narrative, we first need to hone in on one of the most prominent themes in *The Bible*, which is to say, the theme of power. More specifically, we're talking about power derived directly from the blessing of God Himself. In this story of power, we'd do well to note that throughout human history God has always been willing to give power to His chosen vessels, all the while knowing that in time those whom He blesses will inevitably abuse that power and be corrupted by it.

Again and again, whether it's Adam and Eve, or Israel and Judah, the chosen ones begin in a state of blissful ignorance, believing themselves to be God's perpetual darlings. Then, complacency and pride creep in, slowly but surely eroding the established order, followed by disobedience and rebellion. Finally, after all the stern warnings of the Lord are ignored comes His reluctant, though necessary, punishment as depicted in the first couple's fall from grace and the kingdoms of Israel and Judah's deportation into slavery. Yet according to a similarly persistent pattern, God places a time limit on this period of judgment. Instead of destroying the people of His calling, His chastisement ultimately leads to repentance and renewal, thereby bringing them to a higher level of responsibility and awareness.

In the case of Noah's sons after the Flood, then, we have a perfect example of this phenomenon. But in revisiting this story of the corruptibility of God's blessings, we also come face to face with yet another misconception of *The Bible*. That's because when most people think of Nimrod, they generally think of him only in terms of his role in the building of the Tower of Babel. But often overlooked is that while Scripture describes Nimrod as the first great rebel after the Flood, he didn't begin as a rebel. Far from it, in fact. We know this for several reasons—from the testimony of both the canonical and non-canonical record. As it is written:

> Nimrod began to be a mighty one on the Earth. He was a mighty hunter before the Lord; so it's said, "Like Nimrod, a mighty hunter before the Lord."[57]

When reading this text in English, though, it's easy to miss an all-important clue that only becomes apparent when we look to the meaning of the Hebrew word translated here as "before." The word in question is *panim*, which means "to face." According to *Strong's Exhaustive Concordance*, we see this word defined as "facing" in the sense of being "under the watchful eye of, or oversight of." In this context, then, Nimrod wasn't a mighty hunter because he was naturally skilled in the hunt. According

---

57   *Genesis 10:8-9*

to *The Bible*, his skill as a hunter came from his being blessed by God Himself, which is further indicated by the verse that tells us, "So it's said, 'Like Nimrod, a mighty hunter before the Lord.'"

But why he was blessed isn't specified in the canonical record. It can, however, be found in another text similar to that of *First Enoch*. Just as the mystery of why God sent a worldwide deluge was hidden until we found the necessary clues outside of the canonical record, we again find the clue as to why God considered Nimrod worthy of His blessing. According to the parabiblical text called *The Book of Jasher*, we read:

> And God gave Nimrod might and strength, and he was a mighty hunter in the Earth, yes, he was a mighty hunter in the field. And he hunted the animals and he built altars, and he offered upon them the animals before the Lord.
>
> And the Lord delivered all the enemies of his brethren into his hands, and God prospered him from time to time in his battles, and he reigned upon the Earth.
>
> Therefore it became current in those days, when a man ushered forth those whom he'd trained for battle, he'd say to them, "Like God did for Nimrod, who was a mighty hunter in the Earth, and who succeeded in the battles that prevailed against his brethren, that he delivered them from the hands of their enemies, so may God strengthen us and deliver us today."[58]

Only after Nimrod's power became so great, that he consolidated his power with the building of a tower that reached toward Heaven, was God's blessing removed from his life. Only after he united the whole world in one language and instituted idol worship did God finally end the threat with the Confusion of Tongues.

But, really, what did God find so disturbing about Nimrod's efforts on the plain of Shinar that He resorted to such lengths as dividing the people? Was it because Nimrod was the first world ruler to establish idol worship? Was it because he incited

------

58	*Jasher 7:32-33*

a worldwide rebellion against God? Was it because he inspired the people to build a tower toward Heaven?

Again we find the answer in the first book of *The Bible*:

> "Come," they said, "let us build for ourselves a city with a tower that reaches to the heavens, so we can make a name for ourselves and avoid being *scattered* over the face of all the Earth."
>
> Then the Lord came down to see the city and the tower that the sons of men were building, and He said, "If they've begun to do this as one people, speaking the same language, then nothing they devise is beyond them. Come, let Us go down and confuse their language so they won't be able to understand each other anymore.
>
> So the Lord *scattered* them from that place, and they stopped building the city. That's why it's called Babel, because there the Lord confused the language of the whole world, and from there the Lord *dispersed* them into all the Earth.[59]

Whereas the sons of Noah initially intended to obey the command of God, the men of Shinar had other plans. Here we need to be reminded of what I explained earlier about that certain set of Hebrew words that speak of "dividing," "scattering," and "dispersing." Just as the word *parad* spoke of Noah's sons "dispersing" across the face of the Earth, we find a similar Hebrew word employed here. Nimrod and his minions declared they wouldn't be "scattered." The word in this instance, which is very similar, etymologically, to *parad*, is *puwts*. In using this word *puwts*, we see how God had the final word in this scenario, in that Scripture declares: So the Lord "scattered" them, *puwts*, from that place, and "dispersed" them, *puwts*, across the face of the Earth, just as He'd originally commanded them to do.

Apart from the context of God's command to spread out across the face of the Earth, then, we assume the great sin of Nimrod and his people was in their building a tower "to reach the heavens." But in context, we see their real sin was their defiance of God's command to disperse, articulated in their own

---

59 *Genesis 11:4-8*

words as to why they built the tower, which was "to avoid being scattered across the face of the Earth." That's why God did what He did, in confusing their language—not just to thwart their upward movement but, rather, to thwart their movement toward centralization.

And so, by restoring the original division of languages amongst the sons of Noah, God reset His plan once more, and in this great reset, one of the greatest consolidations of power was turned back on its heels. Now, it was possible, finally, for an even greater migration to begin to flow back out and across the face of the whole Earth, as God had originally intended all along.

This Tug of War

SO IN telling the story of the promise of America, technology, and the New World—and in telling it through the prism of God's desire to make Earth more like Heaven—we first have to acknowledge the existence of this tug of war of the ages. It's no less than a back-and-forth struggle between God's willingness to localize His presence and thus to bestow power upon certain humans of His choice, and how those humans inevitably succumb to the corrupting nature of that divine presence and power. Whether in the case of Adam and Eve, or Noah and his children, or Abraham and his family, *The Bible* is the key to understanding how this power struggle has laid the foundation for the history of the world as we know it. In it we find how God intends that the promises He holds out to humanity in every age will survive every effort of the devil and his minions to thwart those promises.

In short, Earth is the battleground, where God and His words of promise and hope are pitted against Satan and his words of doubt and confusion. From that first encounter with Adam and Eve, the devil sowed seeds of doubt and confusion—doubt as to God's goodness and love, confusion as to whether God had really given them all they needed. In opposing everything God has ever promised to humanity, all the devil has ever had to do is interject a subtle yet powerful series of suggestions—innuendos, really: "Did God really mean what He said? Are you sure there isn't more to it than that? Are you sure He's not holding something back? Don't you realize you could be so much more? Don't you know you could be like God, if only you're willing to do whatever it takes?"

And just as it was then, so it is now. Still the war rages on; still the questions linger: Are we content to patiently pray, in the knowledge that God's will is being done, day by day, on Earth as it is in Heaven? Or will we instead brazenly build a tower to Heaven, of our own design, and enter in according to our own schedule?

CHAPTER SEVEN

THE DIVIDING OF THE EARTH

*When the Most High divided their inheritance
to the nations, and when He separated the
sons of Adam, He set the boundaries of the
peoples according to the number of the
Children of Israel. But the Lord's portion is
His people, Jacob is His allotted inheritance.
(Deuteronomy 32:8-9)*

An Ongoing Power Struggle

ONE OF THE most overlooked consequences of the Great Flood was that before that cataclysmic event the geography of the antediluvian world was far different from our own. According to most biblical scholars, before the Flood a single land mass was surrounded by a great ocean. So when the Scriptures describe how the waters above the Earth broke down and the fountains of the deep broke up, the resulting upheaval redistributed this single land mass, and so transformed global geography into what it is today.

Of course critics of *The Bible* deny such a possibility, insisting our present-day geography is the result of many long ages, in which tectonic plates only gradually moved the continents into their current positions. And while evidence of tectonic plate activity exists—in which scientists invoke the term "uniformitarianism"—an honest look at the geological evidence also reveals just as much evidence of abrupt cataclysms throughout Earth's history. For this perspective on Earth science, we're greatly indebted to the pioneering work of men like Georges Cuvier (1768-1832) and Immanuel Velikovsky (1895-1975) who went to great lengths to articulate the theory of "catastrophism" to explain our present-day geography.

And while this present work can't possibly present all the geological evidence to confirm such a position, one thing is certain: In the context of what *The Bible* says about an ongoing power struggle between God, Satan, and humanity, there's little doubt the Flood not only removed the *Nephilim* from the Earth, but it also divided the Earth's land mass into what it is today.

Now, it's also important to note that just as there are opposing views of the dividing of the Earth, in terms of secular versus sacred, there are opposing views within the sacred school as well. The verses in question read as follows:

> This is the account of Noah's sons: Shem, Ham, and Japheth, who also had sons after the Flood... And sons were also born to Shem, the older brother of Japheth. Shem was the forefather of all the sons of Eber... Two sons were born to Eber: One was named Peleg, because in his days the Earth was *divided*, and his brother was named Joktan.[60]

Many times in Scripture a person was named in memory of a special event that occurred in their lifetime. In this case, Peleg, whose name in Hebrew means "division," is so designated. The word used here should look familiar, in that it's similar to the ones I spoke of earlier, in reference to the ongoing theme of dividing, scattering, and uniting. Here, the Hebrew word in question for "divided" is *palag*. And though the reason Eber's son was named Peleg is alluded to, the exact nature of the "dividing" associated with his name isn't spelled out for us, and so has remained a point of debate ever since.

Again, we should never be surprised by this conflict in biblical interpretation, and we shouldn't for the reasons I've already cited: One, God's word is apparently designed this way to force

---

60 *Genesis 10:1, 21, 25*

its readers to decide the meaning for themselves, thus revealing more about the interpreter of the message than the message itself; two, this is always due to the decidedly ambiguous nature of the biblical message; and three, because the message is cleverly couched in paradoxical terms, it inevitably leads us to a crossroad, where we must ask: Is this a genuine paradox or just another inconsistency?

Based on one's interpretation of why Peleg was given this name, then, we might accept any of the following—or combination of—explanations. One, the Earth might have changed from a single land mass to our present-day geography because of a geological event known as the Great Flood. Echoes of this are heard when the chronicler reminded his readers, "Two sons were born to Eber: One was named Peleg, because in his days the Earth was divided."[61] The Hebrew word used here for the "divided" Earth is *palag*.

Two, because Peleg isn't named until four generations after the Flood, this division was the result of not just the breaking up of the Earth but also a later event that caused the seawater to inundate the broken-up geography and create the various oceans as we know them today. We see this same idea when God asked Job: "Who has divided a watercourse for the overflowing of waters."[62] The word for "divided" here, in Hebrew, is *pilag*.

Or three, the land mass was divided first by the breaking up of the Earth's crust, then the encroaching seawater, followed by a cultural event, where the dividing of the languages occurred at the Tower of Babel. Certainly the psalmist had this in mind when he said, "Destroy, oh Lord, and divide their tongues, because I've seen violence and strife in the city."[63] The Hebrew word here for "divide" is *pallag*.

Particularly noteworthy, according to *Strong's Exhaustive Concordance*, this Hebrew word, with its cognates, is only found in three other places in Scripture besides its first occurrence in *The Book of Genesis*. Thus, in *The First Book of Chronicles*, it speaks of dividing the Earth, in *The Book of Job*, it speaks of dividing

---

61   *First Chronicles 1:19*

62   *Job 38:25*

63   *Psalm 55:9*

the waters, and in *The Book of Psalms*, it speaks of dividing the languages. So, regardless of whichever version of this dividing event you embrace, we can be sure of one thing: God was so determined to see to it that the children of Adam went forth to fill the whole Earth, He went to catastrophic lengths to get it done.

No Shortage of Evidence

THAT SAID, I can't help wondering: How many Christians reading this are making the connection that any evangelical mind should have made by now? How many can see that the Great Commission of Christ, in sending His disciples into all the Earth to preach the gospel, is nothing less than a grand continuation of what God has been telling humanity in every age since the days of Adam and Eve? And more importantly, how many discern that the process of dividing, scattering, and uniting hasn't just occurred in the lives of Noah and his immediate family, but is nowhere in history more beautifully exemplified than in this land of the New World called America?

No doubt, though, because traditions are so hard to overcome, even Christians who are aware of the biblical origins of America will resist connecting them with what they read in *The Bible*. Sure, they'd concede the Pilgrims came to this land hoping to create a new society based on the scriptural principles of liberty, justice, and equality. But just because the founders of America were inspired by Scripture doesn't mean anything in Scripture predicted the creation of America. Right?

And that, of course, is where things get interesting. Because while most Christians resist the idea that *The Bible* could have both inspired *and* predicted the creation of America, I must insist that even the most ardent skeptic remain open minded. After all, considering the peculiar circumstances surrounding the formation of our nation, in terms of both secular and sacred history, one actually finds it *harder* to believe that Scripture didn't predict it rather than that it did.

Just consider what we're dealing with when Christians speak of *The Bible*. Isn't it supposed to be a book that tells the history of all the great nations as they pertain to God's plan, as well as of the future world powers that will play a part in the consummation of the ages? If so, then just think about what you're saying when you insist that Scripture failed to foresee the advent of a nation like the United States of America. In this instance, if Scripture drew a blank regarding the advent of America, we'd be talking about a book that foresaw the future of nations but not of one of the most dominating world powers in history. A book that foresaw the future of the world but not of one transformed by America's technology, which has reshaped the Earth more than any other nation known to mankind. And a book that foresaw the arrival of the New Earth, coming down as a bride to greet an awaiting groom, but not of the future world as it will one day become prior to its grand appearance.

Tell me, then, you who claim to believe in the visionary power of Scripture: How does such a possibility speak of an omniscient God, to completely miss the advent of the greatest world power, in conjunction with that other world power, of which it was said the Sun never set on the British Empire? Does that even make sense?

So, rather than continue the tradition of straining out gnats and swallowing camels, the job of truth-seekers is to confront the very real evidence we'd expect to find—and do find—but that has so often been obscured through disinformation. As such, the challenge is to decipher the clues of America's origins, and to once and for all organize them in a coherent, credible manner.

That's why I've begun this deciphering of clues, in the context of the recurring historical narratives that speak of dividing, scattering, and uniting. Yes, to anyone who looks to the evidence of the biblical origins of America, there's no shortage of evidence. Yes, to anyone who looks, there are ample works that connect the people of Scripture with those who found their way to the shores of the New World. But to my knowledge, never have these facts of biblical history been woven together in the context of—what, I believe, has been buried until now—the hidden meaning of the words of Scripture that lie at the heart of this ages-long mystery.

That's why I'll repeatedly speak about the promise of America, technology, and the New Earth in terms of a never-before-told story. While the story of *how* America today is connected to ancient Israel has been told in many ways, this work will constitute the first attempt to explain *why* they're connected.

Their Appointed Times and Boundaries

TO BEGIN the story of *why* ancient Israel and America today are connected, I offer two words from the wise. One is handed down to us from the mouth of Moses, the deliverer of Israel, sometime around 1450 B.C., and the other comes from that of Daniel J. Boorstin, the United States Librarian of Congress, from 1975 to 1987.

First, as the Children of Israel were poised to enter the Promised Land, Moses told them something that had far greater implications than that generation could have ever known at the time. He said:

> When the Most High *divided* their inheritance to the nations, and when He *separated* the sons of Adam, He set the boundaries of the peoples according to the number of the Children of Israel. But the Lord's portion is His people, Jacob is His allotted inheritance.[64]

Second, in speaking of the uniqueness of America, Boorstin pointed to a critical factor that explains why Colonial America succeeded in its early years as a young nation.

> With the settlement of the colonies in North America, for the first time in history the English "provinces" became transatlantic. The story of American civilization gives us an opportunity to see what may happen when a prospering old culture detaches a piece of itself to a great distance. On the other side of a broad ocean the civilization of Englishmen became something it never could have become within their little island...
>
> While Cromwell's army could master next-door Ireland, neither he nor his successors could effectively assert the power of the English Parliament over the transatlantic Americans. Three thousand miles of ocean

---

64   *Deuteronomy 32:8-9*

accomplished what could not be accomplished by a thousand years of history. The Atlantic Ocean proved a more effective advocate than all the constitutional lawyers of Ireland.[65]

Now admittedly, connecting the divided inheritance of the world's nations to the geographical uniqueness of America might seem like quite a leap in logic, but I assure you, it's something that I'll connect in due time. As I've already said, this interplay of dividing, scattering, and uniting will occur so often throughout this work, it will sometimes be difficult to know when one sequence of events has ended and the next one has begun.

This is never more evident than in the following connection of biblical words. When *Genesis* describes the "spreading out" of Noah's sons after the Great Flood, in which the Hebrew word is *parad*, we find that *The Book of Deuteronomy* uses two words that are both derivatives of this same root word—when the Most High "divided" their inheritance to the nations, and when He "separated" the sons of Adam. Of similar interest, when the *King James* Version of *The Bible* uses the alternative word "gave," in reference to this inheritance of the nations, *Strong's Exhaustive Concordance* makes the meaning of this word clear in the Hebrew, where the English does not. In God's "giving" of this inheritance to the nations, it is specifically a giving that speaks of it being "distributed," "apportioned," or "divided" among the various recipients.

To further illustrate this difficulty in knowing when one sequence of events has ended and the next one has begun, let's return to our previous discussion of the scattering of the people at the Tower of Babel.

As you'll recall, I asked: What did God find so disturbing about Nimrod's efforts on the plain of Shinar that He resorted to such lengths as dividing the people? Many assume it was because his tower building was a by-product of Nimrod being the first-recorded world ruler to establish idol worship. Others point

---

65 *Hidden History: Exploring Our Secret Past; The Therapy of Distance, Daniel J. Boorstin, Vintage Books 1987, pp. 65-66*

to his rebellion toward God's rulership so clearly manifested in his stated desire to build a tower that reached to Heaven. Still others insist that Nimrod's real sin was his arrogance in uniting a people that God had gone to such great lengths to diversify. In other words, when God scattered the people at Shinar, it wasn't just to overthrow the building of the tower, or the rebellion of Nimrod, or the practice of idol worship. Certainly, all these things are repugnant to God; but just as certainly God could have punished any of these sins without His dividing the people by confusing their language. He could've called down fire or hail upon them, smitten them with temporary blindness or crippling disease, covered the land in darkness or an impenetrable mist. But He didn't. Instead, God scattered them by confusing their language because by striking at this aspect of their existence, He was effectively reinstating what He'd accomplished when He divided the land mass in the first place, which in turn did so much to encourage the diversity that flourished among Noah's sons after the Flood. As such, God wasn't so much striking at the human tendency toward idol worship or rebellion—which would require a much different solution to solve—as much as He was striking at their consolidation of power.

This becomes clear when we re-examine what God said when He decided to scatter them from the plain of Shinar.

> If they've begun to do this as one people, speaking the same language, then nothing they devise is beyond them.[66]

We'll be repeatedly referring to this subject, of the timeless power struggle between God, Satan, and humanity, just as we'll be repeatedly referring to the interplay of dividing, scattering, and uniting. And as I've said, in doing so, we'll sometimes lose track of where one thread ends and another begins.

That said, we return our attention to how God's dividing of the nations, with the Children of Israel in mind, connects with the geography of America. But in order to do that, it's critical that we keep in mind this thread of the tug of war over power, as elusive of a thread as ever there was one.

---

66 Genesis 11:6

First, we must remember that God is the One Who subverts such power, yet paradoxically, He's also the One Who bestows this power upon whom He chooses. So while it's easy to second guess God in the choices He makes, we'll ultimately find that as the Great Director of human history, He knows exactly what He's doing. In the end, we'll discern the correctness in how He orchestrates not only the history of Earth's geography but also that of the nations. Lose sight of this controlling factor, and you'll find yourself drowning in the same doubt and skepticism that transformed Thomas Paine from Revolutionary America's greatest voice of inspiration into its most vehement voice of cynicism.

So, when we fail to consider why God divided the Earth's land mass, we run the risk of failing to appreciate why God scattered Nimrod's followers. We also run the risk of failing to appreciate why God inspired Moses to inform the Children of Israel that the boundaries of the whole world were laid out with them in mind. And in regard to the promise of America, we also run the risk of failing to appreciate how differently American history would've turned out had it not been for our unique geographical location on Earth.

What's more, not only does Moses tell us that the boundaries of the nations were predetermined according to the Children of Israel, but this same idea is also confirmed in the mouth of two more biblical witnesses. Said the psalmist:

> God is my King from ancient times, working salvation on the Earth. You *divided* the sea by Your strength...
> The day is yours and also the night; You established the Moon and the Sun.
> You have set all the borders of the Earth; You've made summer and winter.[67]

Notice how often here the psalmist drives home ideas so pertinent to this work: God's salvation effort involving the Earth as well as a dividing of the sea. Then there's the occurrence of a similar root word, *parar*, used to describe this "dividing." Then we see the psalmist's emphasis on God's instruments of dividing

---

67   *Psalm 74:12-13, 16-17*

time and space. The Moon and Sun create our experience that divides day from night, and they're involved in the changing of the seasons that divide summer from winter. Finally, we have the way in which Earth's borders divide one nation from another.

No doubt the Apostle Paul, who was so thoroughly steeped in the theology of *The Old Testament*, had all this in mind when he wrote concerning God:

> From one man He made every nation of men, that they should inhabit the whole Earth; and He marked out their appointed times in history and the boundaries of their lands. God did this so that they'd seek Him and perhaps reach out and find Him, though He isn't far from any one of us.[68]

According to Paul's statement, not only are the borders of every nation divinely foreordained, but even the birth and death of those nations are determined by the sovereignty of God. Taken together, the declarations of Moses, the psalmist, and Paul, combined with the peculiar circumstances surrounding the creation of America, remind us of the same persistent paradox. If the Scriptures are that concerned with the history of the nations—sacred and profane, ancient and future—then how could a book full of the prophetic wisdom of the ages ignore a nation like America?

In short, if *The Bible* is brimming with the paradoxical nature of God's truth, and Jesus, the Incarnate word of God, is a walking, talking paradox, then doesn't it stand to reason that the paradox that is America finds its origins there, too?

---

68 *Acts 17:26-27*

CHAPTER EIGHT

THE PARADOX THAT IS AMERICA

*You ignored the Rock Who brought you forth;
you forgot the God Who gave you birth. When
the Lord saw this, He rejected them ... and said,
"They've provoked My jealousy by that which
is not God ... so I'll make them jealous by those
who are not a people; I'll make them angry by
a nation without understanding."(Deuteronomy
32:18-19, 21)*

A New Wilderness Experience

AMERICA—the land of "one out of many"—is the very definition of a paradox. A land that's unique yet universal, rooted in time yet timeless, born through an idea yet unleashed through technology. It began as a land sought out as a source of fabulous wealth and riches, a place that inevitably brought out the worst in mankind—greed, robbery, and murder. Yet, in time, it became a land sought out as a refuge for truth, justice, and freedom—a place that elevates the human soul to unparalleled heights.

What's more, it's a land that owes its existence to a people who were fleeing religious persecution, yet a land that could never have fulfilled its destiny had Americans not freed themselves from the darker aspects of the philosophy of those who spawned it.

It's a land built upon an idea inspired by *The Bible*—as "a city upon a hill"—yet it would never have endured to this day if it hadn't separated itself from the very idea that inspired it. A land that's the fulfillment of some of the most important biblical promises concerning the destiny of the Earth, yet born of a promise that points to that future day when we'll witness the appearance of a new Earth prepared as a bride beautifully adorned for her husband.

This is the story of the paradox that is America.

At the crossroads of history, where the British, Scots, Irish, Dutch, French, Spanish, Portuguese, Scandinavians, Italians, Germans, Africans, and others all came together in new ways, America was also the place where the ancient conflicts of the Old World would be reworked and disarmed. Not unlike many New World civilizations, America was scarred by racism, bigotry, and slavery, yet it never ceased to be the crucible where these universal ills were faced head-on and laid to rest in a uniquely American quest for "liberty and justice for all."

Unlike other nations whose origins reach too far into the past to offer any certainty about their origins, America is a land whose birth is so recent that it can be pointed to with historical precision. Yet upon further examination, America is also a land whose origins will reveal a far more ancient starting point than typically believed.

The first nation to be established merely on the foundation of an idea, America, because of a new way of acting upon ideas—born of the necessities of its time and place in history—is also a land that became synonymous with the spirit of invention, industry, and technology.

A land free to fully embrace the ideas of men like John Locke, Roger Williams, and Montesquieu, who provided new insights about how humane, just governments should act, it was also a place where those ideas could be reshaped as the need arose for this new society, forged out of a new wilderness experience called America.

Ironically, then, though we associate the Pilgrims with the spirit of religious freedom, the reality is they weren't so much seeking freedom of conscience as they were seeking freedom from the abuses of the State-run Church in England.

Far from seeking religious independence for its own sake, New England Puritans soon began a similar politicizing of their new society, which was actually a continuation of the same societal forces that caused them to flee Old England in the first place. Had it not been for men and women of courage and enlightenment, in response to a new Puritan aristocracy, American history, with its special creed of freedom of worship and liberty of conscience, would have turned out much differently from the one we know today.

This, then, is the story of the paradox that is America.

It is the story of *a* people, and the story of *all* people. It's also the pursuit of *a* people, and the pursuit of *all* people, people who desperately seek yet rarely find what they seek—the freedom to *think* as they choose, the freedom to *live* as they choose, the freedom to *be* as they choose.

It is the story of a people who set out upon a timeless quest ... in 1492 ... in 1620 ... in 1776. It's also the story of another people, in a long distant past, a people who resided deep in the memory of those later people, who were just as eager, just as plagued by doubt as any who've ever wandered the face of the Earth.

The Call to Remembrance

THE AIMLESS wandering of the Children of Israel was finally coming to an end. After forty years, Moses and his two faithful companions Joshua and Caleb were all that was left of the original group that had escaped Egyptian bondage. An entire generation—an estimated two to three million souls—was now dead and buried, all eyewitnesses to the ten plagues that assaulted the Egyptians, in God's efforts to induce Pharaoh to let His people go.

Now only their children and their children's children continued to march onward, even as the lingering question haunted them in this last leg of their decades-long journey to the Promised Land: How could a God so powerful, in miraculously freeing us from Egyptian slavery, lack the ability to bring our parents into this land so they could also enjoy the fruits of that freedom?

Yet even as the question lingered, so did the answer—bittersweet as that answer was then, even as it is now. Even now, the answer of why a generation miraculously delivered by God was both blessed and cursed is obvious, because it's always easier to understand the past from the vantage point of the present. Looking back, what seemed so mysterious to the children who were still alive seems clear to us. That's because the most important element in understanding those events is that, in hindsight, we see what happened to them was never meant for their sakes alone. In short, God intended that wilderness experience to reveal a universal truth to all those who are similarly called from time to time, as outsiders, outliers, and aliens, like father Abraham before them, led forth from the confines of this darkened world.

So for anyone who has ever heard the tale of those wilderness wanderers, let the lesson of their lives speak to your own situation today, just as it spoke to the disciples of Jesus in their day. No doubt the disciples had been weaned on the story of those feckless wanderers who squandered the grace of God after having witnessed so many of God's miracles at the hand of Moses. And for any of us who insists we'd do things differently than those wandering Israelites, demanding more than manna and miracles, differently than those disciples of Jesus, seeking more than bread and forgiveness, think again, because you and I are made of the very same stuff as them.

It's not too hard to imagine how the memory of those wandering Israelites might have run through the minds of the disciples, even as they sought to persuade Jesus to do more than turn water into wine or calm the storm with but a word. Did the hard lesson of that generation invade their thoughts long enough to remind them of what happens when God's people turn His calling into something other than what He intends it to be? And like them, will we heed the call to remembrance, of the tragic events of that stubborn generation?

No sooner had those Israelites departed from Egypt than they found themselves trapped, smack dab between the Red Sea and Pharaoh's pursuing army. But rather than remember what

God and His servant Moses had done to extricate them, they groaned:

> "Was it because there were no graves in Egypt that you brought us into the Wilderness to die? What have you done to us by bringing us out here? Didn't we tell you in Egypt, 'Leave us alone so we can serve the Egyptians'? For it would've been better for us to serve the Egyptians than to die in the Wilderness."
>
> But Moses told the people, "Don't be afraid. Stand firm and you'll see the Lord's salvation, which He'll accomplish for you today; because the Egyptians you see today, you'll never see again. The Lord will fight for you; you need only to be still."[69]

Of course we all know what happened next, right? Moses raised his staff, the Red Sea parted, the Israelites walked to the other side as if they were on dry land, and when Pharaoh's army pursued them, the waters came crashing down on the Egyptians and drowned them all.

> So that day the Lord saved Israel from the hand of the Egyptians, and Israel saw the Egyptians dead on the shore. When Israel saw the great power that the Lord had exercised over the Egyptians, the people feared the Lord and believed in Him and in His servant Moses.[70]

That is to say, the people feared the Lord and believed in Him and in His servant Moses ... for a while.

Just three days removed from the Red Sea, the people began to complain to Moses that there was no water. Immediately God had Moses lead them to two sources of water, first at Marah, where God sweetened waters that were originally too bitter to drink, and then to Elim, where the people found twelve wells from which to drink...

Soon after, they began complaining that because

---

69   Exodus 14:11-14

70   Ibid. 14:30-31

there was no food to be found God might as well have left them to die in Egypt where they at least didn't have to contend with empty bellies. In response to their grumblings, God sent vast numbers of quail into their midst to feed them. Not only that, but He also provided them with a peculiar substance known as *manna*, a kind of bread that tasted like honey-filled wafers, which grew out of the ground like a plant, with which the people satisfied their hunger.[71]

The ironic thing about this series of events is, in hindsight it's obvious to us that the Lord was testing the faith of this fickle bunch of exiles. One minute the Israelites are about to be killed by Pharaoh's pursuing army, the next minute the Red Sea collapses on them and they're happy with God—for a while, that is.

Then, no sooner are they past the next series of trials, having been provided for with sweetened water, twelve wells, quail, and *manna*, the people find themselves without water yet again. But instead of giving God the benefit of the doubt, by having faith in Him and His ordained leader, what did they do?

The people began to chide with Moses, saying, "How about giving us more water to drink?"

And Moses replied, "Why are you giving me such a hard time? You're only irritating God with your belligerence!"

But the people were so thirsty that they continued to press the matter, saying, "Is this why you brought us out of Egypt? So you could kill us and our cattle with thirst?"

So Moses begged God: "What should I do with these people? They all want to stone me!"

And the Lord told Moses: "Take the rod with which you parted the Red Sea and strike the Rock in the sight of everyone."

And water came forth from the Rock to quench the thirst of the Israelites. That's why Moses named that place Meribah, (which means *provocation* or *strife*) be-

---

71   *Exodus 15:22-27; 16:3-36*

cause that's where the Israelites questioned whether or not the Lord was still with them.[72]

As the Israelites ventured further and further away from their old home, they encountered challenges they could've met with courage and tenacity, considering all they'd seen God do on their behalf. But they didn't. No wonder God got fed up, as *The Book of Hebrews* records:

> Today if you hear God's voice, don't harden your hearts, as it was in the day of provocation, in the Wilderness when your forefathers tempted Me, proved Me, and saw My works for forty years. And because of what they did to Me there, I was grieved with that generation, saying, "Their hearts are always in error regarding My ways, so I swore in My anger they wouldn't enter into My rest."[73]

And again:

> With whom was God grieved for forty years? Wasn't it with those who sinned, whose carcasses fell in the Wilderness? And to those whom He swore they wouldn't enter into His rest, that is to say, those who wouldn't believe? So we see they couldn't enter in because of a lack of faith."[74]

Instead of maturing toward greater levels of faith, instead of graduating to new heights of trust, those stubborn Israelites degraded month by month and year by year. Eventually, God grew so weary with them He had no choice but to lead them in circles through the Wilderness until that embittered generation died off, leaving only Moses, Joshua, Caleb, and everyone under twenty years of age.

The Fate of This Present World

WHEN THE long-awaited day arrived, at the end of their forty-year wandering, Moses and the next generation of Israelites

---

72   Exodus 17:1-7

73   Hebrews 3:7-11

74   Ibid. 3:17-19

stood at the edge of the Promised Land. In honor of the event, Moses wrote a special song for the people, summing up all that led up to that day and what they should expect from that point on. Comprised of more than forty verses, *The Song of Moses* is condensed here for the sake of brevity:

I will proclaim the name of the Lord, and ascribe greatness to our God! He is the Rock, His work is perfect; all His ways are just. A God of faithfulness without injustice, righteous and upright is He...

Isn't He your Father and Creator? Didn't He make you and establish you? Remember the days of old; consider the years long past. Ask your fathers, and they'll tell you, your elders, and they'll inform you. When the Most High *divided* their inheritance to the nations, and when He *separated* the sons of Adam, He set the boundaries of the peoples according to the number of the Children of Israel. But the Lord's portion is His people, Jacob is His allotted inheritance.

God found him in a desert land, in a barren, howling wilderness; He surrounded him, He instructed him, He guarded him as the apple of His eye. As an eagle stirs up its nest and hovers over its young, He spread His wings to catch them and carried them on His pinions. The Lord alone led him, and no foreign god was with him...

But Jeshurun (My Upright One, My Israel) grew fat and kicked—becoming bloated and gorged. He abandoned the God Who made him and scorned the Rock of his salvation...

You ignored the Rock Who brought you forth; you forgot the God Who gave you birth. When the Lord saw this, He rejected them; provoked to anger by His sons and daughters, He said: "I will hide My face from them. I'll see what their end will be. For they're a perverse generation—children of unfaithfulness. They've provoked My jealousy by that which is not God; they've enraged Me with their worthless idols. So I'll make them jealous by those who are not a people; I'll make them angry by a nation without understanding."[75]

For anyone interested in the purpose and destiny of God's people, one need look no further than *The Song of Moses*. It explains why, of all the nations of the Earth, the descendants of Abraham's grandson Jacob are so blessed and so cursed, why they've attained the greatest of destinies and the saddest of predicaments. Fortunately for them—and for us—the story doesn't end in despair but rather in redemption. As Moses had God continue to say:

> "I'd have said that I would cut them to pieces and blot out their memory from mankind, if I hadn't dreaded the taunt of the enemy, lest their adversaries misunderstand, and say: 'Our own hand has prevailed; it wasn't the Lord Who did all this.' Israel is a nation devoid of counsel, with no understanding among them. If only they were wise … they'd comprehend their fate..."
>
> For the Lord will vindicate His people and have compassion on His servants when He sees that their strength is gone and no one remains, slave or free...
>
> And God said, "See now that I am He; there's no God besides Me. I bring death and I give life; I wound and I heal, and there's no one who can deliver from My hand..."
>
> Rejoice, oh heavens, with Him, and let all God's angels worship Him. Rejoice, oh nations, with His people; for He'll avenge the blood of His children. He'll take vengeance on His adversaries and repay those who hate Him; He'll cleanse His land and His people.[76]

For anyone interested in the fate of this present world, and of America in particular, I contend the preceding verses provide all the ingredients we need to grasp what I hope to convey in this work, in which I'll set forth God as:

1) The Rock of Salvation, as faithful Father and Creator.

---

75   *Deuteronomy 32:3-4, 6-12, 15, 18-21*

76   *Ibid. 32:26-29, 36, 39, 43*

2) The Most High Who divided the world so that even before the sons of Adam began to multiply across the face of the Earth, the boundaries of humanity were already set according to the number of the Children of Israel.

3) The One Who chose Jacob as His allotted inheritance, Who found Israel in a barren wilderness, surrounded him, instructed him, and guarded him as the apple of His eye.

4) The One Who was then rejected by Jeshurun (God's Upright One, His Israel) after he'd grown fat, bloated, gorged, and then abandoned the God Who'd made him, and scorned the Rock of his salvation.

5) The One Who, in response to being rejected by Israel, then rejected them by hiding His face from them. Then, because they provoked Him to jealousy by that which was not God, He chose to make them jealous by those who were not a people; having enraged Him with their worthless idols, He sought to make them angry by a nation without understanding.

6) The One Who chose to not blot out the memory of Israel from mankind, because He dreaded the taunt of the enemy, lest their adversaries misunderstand and think that they'd prevailed over them through their own power.

7) The One Who, while seeing His chosen people, a nation devoid of counsel, with no understanding among them, while seeing that their strength was gone, then determined to avenge the blood of His children, take vengeance on His adversaries, repay those who hate Him, and cleanse His land and His people.

As we proceed further and further along in our story of God's expanding Empire, one can't help but be startled at the turn of events as they unfold. When most of us consider the tug of war of power in *The Bible*, we usually think of those who stand for God and good, like Noah and his faithful followers, warring against those who stand for Satan and evil, like Nimrod and his rebellious minions. It is in this context that we also think of Nebuchadnezzar's Great Image, which represented the various nations, like Babylon, Medo-Persia, Greece, and Rome, that warred against Judah. And it's the context of the struggle between nations that calls our attention to the arrival of the other great kingdom, that of stone, which biblical historians and theologians have yet to identify with the same certainty as those kingdoms of gold, silver, bronze, and iron.

However, even more important to the biblical narrative than the conflict between God and the various personifications of evil is the one between God and the very people He's chosen and set apart for His purposes on Earth. The former conflict is straightforward and obvious while the latter constitutes one of the great mysteries of biblical history. Add to that our typical doubt and skepticism, despite God's word clearly providing us with clue after clue, and the mystery only grows more mysterious.

But to those who are willing to pay attention to these biblical clues, the mystery can't help but reveal its true meaning. Thus, in trying to arrive at a connection between Israel of old and the birth of America, it should be noted that while Israel failed to live up to its full potential, God made it clear through the mouth of Moses that He had no intention of failing. That's because while many of God's promises are conditional by nature and require obedience on the part of the recipients, many more of His promises are unconditional by nature and so come to fruition regardless of the human actors involved.

Case in point: Although Israel of old was given every opportunity to live up to God's call, it grew overconfident and presumptuous in that calling. Having grown fat, bloated, and gorged, Israel abandoned God and scorned the Rock of salvation. Nevertheless, the Rock will not be denied; God's purposes in the Earth will not fail, even when His chosen ones fail to do their part. When Israel provoked God to jealousy by that which was not God, He determined to make them jealous by those who are not a people; and when Israel enraged Him with their worthless idols, God determined to make them angry by a nation without understanding. Certainly Jesus had this in mind when He said to Judah of old:

> So I tell you that the Kingdom of God will be taken from you and given to a nation that will bear fruit. He who falls on this stone will be broken to pieces, but he on whom it falls will be crushed.[77]

That said, could this nation, receiving the Kingdom of God, be the same Stone Kingdom that Daniel predicted would not only destroy the Great Image of Nebuchadnezzar but also fill the whole Earth? If so, then how might we prove that this fruit-bearing kingdom—this stone that crushes—is the same one so indebted to that original Kingdom of Israel? And finally, how might we demonstrate a clear and obvious historical continuity between this Stone Kingdom, Israel of old, and America?

The Tiniest of Actions

AGAIN AND again, *The Bible* employs the metaphor of stone, even though we might assume that when the God of Heaven invoked the idea of stones it would involve stones we associate with precious gems, like diamonds, rubies, or sapphires, or at the very least, gold or silver. After all, isn't that why Scripture had one of the Wise Men present the Christ Child with an offering of gold? Yet more often than not when *The Bible* speaks of the establishment of God's Kingdom on Earth, it's not made up of precious stones that humans value but, rather, ordinary everyday stones. That this is so is yet another of the great paradoxes of Scripture.

Think of how often the use of stone is mentioned when certain ones in the biblical narrative commemorate special events which they believe speak of their unique encounter with God. After Jacob dreamed of a ladder to Heaven, he anointed the rock on which he'd rested his head during the night, and called it the House of God.[78] At Shechem, Joshua raised a pillar of

---

77 Matthew 21:43-44

78 Genesis 28:10-22, 35:1-15

stone as a shrine to the Lord.[79] The Israelites built a temple of uncarved stones.[80] At Sinai, Moses set up twelve standing stones by an altar,[81] and at Gilgal, Joshua followed suit with twelve standing stones.[82] And of course it should be remembered how Elijah, in defiance of Jezebel and her prophets of Baal, built an altar with twelve stones according to the number of the tribes of the sons of Jacob.[83]

All of this, naturally, harkens back to when God, the Outsider, asked Abraham, the outsider, to take his son Isaac to Mount Moriah, there to offer him up upon an altar of stone. Until then, God was still—judicially speaking—an alien in the affairs of humanity. Not that He wasn't still the omnipotent God of the Universe. But sadly, what good is it creating humans in order to have fellowship with them, when God is barred from having that fellowship because of His own divine decree?

Here we are again facing another paradox of Scripture: The Creator God made human beings in His own image, but because Adam bequeathed himself to the devil, the only way God could legally relate to mankind was as a father who could only watch his children from afar because a judge handed down a restraining order prohibiting anything more between the father and his children.

But all that changed when God called Abraham to leave his father's home; and because Abraham obeyed that call, the Lord led him to an unknown land and blessed him with a child of promise. Then, because Abraham willingly raised the sacrificial knife to slay his true born son, that very moment Isaac became a dead man to this world and the devil. So, when God staid the hand of Abraham and spared Isaac that day, from that point onward God *legally* regained entrance back into the stream of human affairs.

That's the real significance of the Binding of Isaac, because that was the day when Abraham and Sarah became the father

---

79   *Joshua 24:22-27*

80   *Exodus 20:25*

81   *Ibid. 24:3-8*

82   *Joshua 4:19-24*

83   *First Kings 18:31-32*

and mother of a new way of life. Like a second Adam and Eve, they became the first parents of faith—the kind of faith that God had hoped the first Adam and Eve might have offered Him. And in this most unexpected way, the tiniest of actions paradoxically laid the foundation for the mightiest nation that the world would ever know—a company of nations, actually.

Ever since then, God has been able to proceed with a brand-new thing on the Earth; it was the beginning of a new covenantal relationship with the descendants of Isaac. And so it was that the Kingdom of Stone came to be established, which began as the tiniest seed of the mustard tree, destined not only to one day destroy the kingdoms of this world but also to fill the whole Earth.

CHAPTER NINE

THESE DUST~LIKE DESCENDANTS

And God said to Abram, "I'll make your
offspring like the dust of the Earth, so if
anyone can count the dust, then your
offspring can be counted... As for Me, this is
My covenant with you: You'll be the father of
many nations. No longer will you be called
Abram; your name will be Abraham, because
I've made you a father of many nations... As
for Sarai your wife, you're no longer to call
her Sarai; her name will be Sarah, because
I'll bless her ... so that she'll be the mother of
nations; kings of peoples will come from her."
(Genesis 13:16; 17:4-5, 15-16)

A Place for My People Israel

IN CONNECTING the history of the Stone Kingdom, Israel, and America, we need to address several questions in relation to the various ingredients I've already mentioned: First, is our current understanding of the "number of the Children of Israel" adequate to this task? Second, if it's not adequate, as I'm contending, then how do we overhaul this flawed view to arrive at a correct numbering of Israel? Third, if Scripture is our source for answers, as it should be, then what clues do we find there to locate the Children of Israel in today's world? Fourth, to which nation, described as "not a people" and "without understanding," is Moses referring, by which God intends to make Israel of old jealous and angry? Fifth, when God spoke of avenging His children and cleansing His land, where might this take place and on behalf of which people? Sixth, is it possible that this nation "without understanding," which Moses described, has any connection with the Kingdom of Stone that Daniel foresaw? And seventh, if there is a connection, then how does this tie into God's plan that the Earth is not to be abandoned but rather—as Jesus taught us to pray—transformed prior to the advent of the New Earth?

As for our first question, whether our current understanding of the number of the Children of Israel is up to this task, let's be clear: While most Christians insist these Israelites comprise the modern Jewish state that was, in 1948, re-established in their ancient homeland of Palestine, this view is dashed to pieces when we look to *The Bible*. Within its pages, we come face to face with yet another of those paradoxical truths we constantly confront when investigating all things biblical. That's because it involves one of the most famous promises of God in Scripture, one that most Christians and Jews alike are aware of, yet without their ever coming to grips with the obvious implications of that promise. And it goes as follows.

The progenitors of the Israelite people are, as we all know, Abraham, of Ur of the Chaldees, and his wife, Sarah. Abraham's name means "father of a multitude," and Sarah's name means "princess." However, long before Abraham became a father of anyone, he and his wife Sarah struggled for many years to have children. An often-overlooked aspect of these two is that before God ever uttered the promise in question, their names were not Abraham and Sarah; they were Abram and Sarai. This is critically important because in *The Bible* names are much more significant than they are in today's world. Names in Scripture often had an uncanny way of revealing the destiny of that person. When Jacob was born, it's said he was grasping the heel of his twin brother Esau, so the midwife suggested the name Jacob, which means "heel-catcher" or "usurper." Certainly Esau on more than one occasion testified to the accuracy of such a name when Jacob twice tricked him out of his father's birthright.

In the case of Abram and Sarai, Abram's name meant "exalted father," because Abram was born to his father Terah at a time when—according to *The Book of Jasher*—Terah had been elevated to chief prince in the court of Nimrod. As for Sarai, while it's true her name is rooted in the same Hebrew word as her new name, an alternate meaning to her original name can mean "contentious" or "stubborn." This is borne out in light of Sarai's initial response to God's promise concerning the birth of her son while still in the grips of her decades-long barrenness. But before we get too far ahead of the story, we have to first learn of the unique beginnings of this multitude of descendants.

When we consider the story of how Abram became Abraham, the question naturally arises: How did he have faith in the God of Heaven while the rest of the world was so steeped in idolatry and rebellion? *The Book of Genesis* records, in the sparsest of terms, that God called Abram to leave his father's house and travel to an unknown land, and in response, the patriarch simply followed that call.[84]

But what really happened to prepare his mind to perceive this call from a God Who had been summarily rejected by the rest of humanity? Concerning this most important question, the canonical record is strangely silent. Certainly you'd think that just such a question would arise in the mind of anyone who'd wish to follow in the footsteps of Abraham. After all, the Apostle Paul declared that those who have faith in God are to be counted as spiritual children of Abraham.[85] If so, then wouldn't it behoove Moses—in his depiction of the formative years of this pioneer of faith—to reveal what enabled Abraham to grasp what no one else could at the time? You'd definitely think so.

Yet only the apocryphal record provides an answer to this mystery. In *The Book of Jasher*, we find that long before Abram went to live with his idol-worshiping father he was forced into exile, where he was nurtured for forty years in the home of none other than Shem and Noah, who together taught the young man

---

84   *Genesis 12:1-4*

85   *Romans 4:11-25*

about the true God.[86] That's why Abram was able to develop a genuine faith in God. That's why his heart and mind were prepared for the call of God when it came. Too bad, then, that this all-important aspect of Abram's early training has been obscured by centuries of misinformation that would tritely attempt to inspire faith in God by telling us that we "just gotta believe."

Of course, this isn't the first example of important aspects of the lives of the giants of faith that are conspicuously absent from the traditional biblical record. In this, the hidden years of Abram's early life foreshadow the so-called "missing years" of Jesus, Who was also forced to flee His homeland so that He, too, could grow up as an outsider, under the care and tutelage of another. So, just as Shem and Noah cared for young Abram in his formative years, Joseph of Arimathea similarly watched over young Jesus until the time came that He was ready to take up the mantle of God's call for His life.

But before Abram rose to embrace that high calling, he was simply the infant son of Terah, chief prince of Nimrod. Furthermore, in an event that prefigured the birth of Jesus, a celestial occurrence took place on the day of Abram's birth, which triggered the malicious actions of the king in that time.[87] In Abram's case, it was Nimrod who, upon the advice of his soothsayers and sages, tried to eliminate the child of destiny from ever growing up to fulfill a prophecy that pronounced the end of his mighty kingdom.[88] But hoping to save the life of his fated son, Terah risked the wrath of his king by bringing him another child—one born to him from his union with a concubine—and it was this child that was killed instead of the infant Abram.[89]

Following the death of this substitute child, Abram—like Jesus Who was also spared when His parents fled the wrath of Herod and hid Him in Egypt—became an exile from his homeland, far removed from the threat seeking to kill him.[90] And just as Jesus had been sheltered in His formative years, the young

---

86   *Jasher 9:4-6*

87   *Ibid. 8:2-4*

88   *Ibid. 8:15-16*

89   *Ibid. 8:33-34*

90   *Ibid. 8:35-36*

son of Terah was spirited away to the mountain fastness of Noah and Shem, where he was secretly mentored for forty years concerning the things of the true God.[91]

Then, many years later, while Abram and Sarai journeyed as strangers and pilgrims through the land of Canaan, God, the Outsider, spoke to Abram, the outsider:

> Look all around you, Abram, to the north and south, to the east and west. All the land that you see, I will give to you and your offspring forever. I'll make your offspring like the dust of the Earth, so if anyone can count the dust, then your offspring can be counted. Go, walk the length and breadth of the land, because I'm giving it to you.[92]

Here we encounter the first of God's promises to Abram regarding the number of his promised descendants, which were to one day be as numerous as the dust of the Earth. Without trying too hard to compute such a number, presently, please reserve this idea firmly in your mind as we proceed.

Of course, from a purely human perspective, the notion that Abram would become the father of many nations seemed ludicrous to say the least. That's because some twenty-five years after God first promised Abram concerning these dust-like descendants, Abram's wife was still childless. Never mind that Sarai had concocted her own scheme to help God keep His promises to Abram. Never mind that, in fixing up her husband with her handmaiden Hagar, the union produced Abram's first child by the name of Ishmael. Never mind that Ishmael was also destined to father a great nation of his own. Because despite all of Sarai's well-intentioned efforts, nothing she did added to God's promises, which pertained exclusively to Abram's offspring through her.

> When Abram was ninety-nine years old, the Lord appeared to him and said, "I am God Almighty; walk before Me faithfully and sincerely. Then I'll make My

---

91   *Jasher 9:5-6*

92   *Genesis 13:14-17*

covenant between Me and you, and I'll greatly increase your numbers."

Abram fell face-down, and God said to him, "As for Me, this is My covenant with you: You'll be the father of many nations. No longer will you be called Abram; your name will be Abraham, because I've made you a father of many nations. I'll make you very fruitful; I'll make nations of you, and kings will come from you. I'll establish My covenant as an everlasting covenant between Me and you and your descendants for generations to come, to be your God and the God of your descendants. The whole land of Canaan, where you now reside as a foreigner, I'll give as an everlasting possession to you and your descendants after you; and I'll be their God..."

God also said to Abraham, "As for Sarai your wife, you're no longer to call her Sarai; her name will be Sarah, because I'll bless her and will certainly give you a son by her. I'll bless her so that she'll be the mother of nations; kings of peoples will come from her."[93]

Here we're faced with a troubling inconsistency, though not so much an inconsistency as another paradox.

As for the inconsistent aspect, we find, in the space of just two passages in *Genesis*, God promising that Abraham will be the father of dust-like descendants, many nations, and kings of peoples. Yet ask the typical believer of Scripture if they honestly believe that God meant what He said here, and even they might blush with embarrassment as they try in vain to convince you the modern-day Jewish people have fulfilled these promises.

Can the number of the people of the modern Jewish state be compared to dust? Is the modern Jewish state comprised of many nations? And is the modern Jewish state presided over by a king born of Abraham and Sarah? Of course, all of these are rhetorical questions, all of which elicit a response of: "No, no, and no." That said, then, the Jewish people inhabiting modern-day Palestine can't possibly be those spoken of as the "number of the Children of Israel."

---

93 *Genesis 17:1-8, 15-16*

What's more, if the promises to Abraham, concerning these descendants, nations, and kings weren't fulfilled by the modern Jewish state, then how do we respond to the accusation that God is therefore a liar, a fraud, or incapable of keeping His promises? Certainly this is what Thomas Paine, that most excellent author of the American Revolution, concluded when he looked at these same circumstances. In fact, this inconsistency so disturbed Paine that although he began his career writing *Common Sense*, which did so much to inspire Colonial America in its revolutionary effort, he became disillusioned by God's apparent failure to keep His word to the Israelites and fell headlong into agnosticism. So much so that Paine went on to pen the most cynical of all revolutionary works, The *Age of Reason,* which had more to do with the Enlightenment thinking that produced France's failed attempt at duplicating the American Revolution. Far from creating a "more perfect union" in post-Revolutionary France, such cynicism instead produced The Reign of Terror.

Just One Man

HAVING LOOKED at the inconsistent aspect of these promises, in regard to how most Christians interpret them, let's turn next to how they should be understood in terms of their paradoxical nature. Remember how we previously defined a paradox: A paradox is "an apparently contradictory statement that, when investigated or explained, may actually prove to be true." In this case, I'd suggest that by facing the truth contained in these passages we're reminded of why God's word is so full of apparent contradictions. That's because built within them are hidden nuggets of truth just waiting to be mined by anyone who is willing to push beyond the apparent inconsistencies in order to embrace what is buried there in the form of a paradox.

In this case, what we see, if we're willing to see, is: While most modern thinkers, Christian and non-Christian alike, find it difficult to accept that God is still in the business of guiding individuals and nations, these passages fly directly in the face of that idea. What's more, for those who are willing to see: These passages actually form the basis of a major turning point in human history as God, the Great Outsider, established here a new relationship with fallen humanity, in order to reverse the downward influence of satanic dominion.

So, when skeptics and critics insist that the God of all people would never concern Himself with the descendants of just one man, we can point to these passages where God says, "I will make My covenant between Me and you, Abraham, and I will greatly increase your numbers." When they insist that the God of all nations would never concern Himself with the nations descended from just one man, we can point to where God says, "I will establish My covenant as an everlasting covenant between Me and you, Abraham, and your descendants for generations to come, to be your God and the God of your descendants." And when they insist that the King of Heaven would never concern Himself with the kings reigning over peoples descended from just one man, we point to where God says, "I will make you very fruitful, Abraham; I'll make nations of you, and kings will come from you."

In all these ways, then, the omnipotent, the omniscient, the omnipresent God reveals His willingness to localize His presence and power in order to stoop down to rescue fallen humanity from the grip of darkness, disease, and death. And while the majority of mankind resists such a grand possibility, these passages will, if given a chance through historical analysis and investigation, prove to be the ultimate touchstone in proving that God is no liar and no fraud. When God states His intentions, He doesn't change His mind; when God makes promises to someone, He always makes good on those promises.

That's why it's so important that we never avoid this issue concerning these tripartite foundational promises of God. And while many admit that their candidate for the fulfillment of these promises lack two of the three indicators of this people of Israel—that of their dust-like numbers and their producing many nations—they still insist that many kings have arisen from the nation of the Jews. That's because *The Bible* does record a long line of Israelite kings, from Saul to Zedekiah. The only problem with that proposition is, the promises of God don't just encompass those made to Abraham in his lifetime. They also include promises made to Abraham's descendants, each in their own turn.

To King David, then, God not only confirmed his kingship over Israel, but through the mouth of Nathan, the prophet, He amplified His original promise to Abraham:

Now then, you're to tell My servant David, this is what the Lord of Hosts says: "I took you from the pasture, from following the flock, to be the ruler of My people Israel. I've been with you wherever you've gone, and I've cut off all your enemies from before you. Now I'll make your name like the greatest in the land.

"And I'll provide a place for My people Israel and will plant them so they can live in a place of their own and be disturbed no more. No longer will the sons of wickedness oppress them as they did at the beginning and have done since the day I appointed judges over My people Israel. I'll give you rest from all your enemies…

"I'll personally establish a house for you. And when your days are fulfilled and you rest with your fathers, I'll raise up your descendant after you, who will come from your own body, and I'll establish his kingdom. He'll build a house for My name, and I'll establish the throne of his kingdom forever. I'll be his Father, and he'll be My son. When he does wrong, I'll discipline him with the rod of men and with the blows of the sons of men.

"But My loving devotion will never be removed from him as I removed it from Saul, whom I moved out of your way. Your house and kingdom will endure forever before Me, and your throne will be established forever."[94]

In other words, the kings who are descended from Abraham and Sarah aren't just going to enter the stage of world history and then exit stage left, never to be seen or heard from again. If God's promises are true and sure, then these dust-like descendants of Abraham and Sarah, who are to comprise many nations, will also have kings and queens who rule and reign over them for all time.

---

94 *Second Samuel 7:8-15*

CHAPTER TEN

HIS LINE WILL CONTINUE FOREVER

*Who can count the dust of Jacob, and the
number of the fourth part of Israel? Speaking of
this time one day, it will be said of Jacob and of
Israel: What has God wrought! How lovely are
your tents, oh Jacob, and your tabernacles, oh
Israel! Like valleys they spread out, like gardens
beside a river, like aloes planted by the Lord,
like cedars beside the waters. He will pour the
water out of his buckets, and his seed will be
in many waters, and his king will be higher
than Agag, and his kingdom will be exalted.
(Numbers 23:10, 23; 24:5-7)*

A Perpetual Earthly Kingship

TWO THINGS arise from—what I'm calling—the tripartite foundational promises of God that are so critical to our investigation. One has immediate application, while the other will provide an important detail later in this discussion.

First, in addition to the dust-like descendants of Abraham and the many nations they are to comprise, God's promise to King David made it equally clear: The kings coming from the loins of his forefather are to reign over Abraham's descendants from an earthly throne that's to be established forever. The psalmist confirmed this when he had God saying:

I won't violate My covenant or alter what My lips have uttered. Once and for all, I've sworn by My holiness; I won't lie to David. His line will continue forever and his throne will endure before Me like the Sun; it will be established forever like the Moon, the faithful witness in the sky.[95]

Now, when it comes to the typical response as to whether or not this promise of God has been fulfilled, the first thing one hears is, this promise doesn't have to be fulfilled in a perpetual earthly kingship. It can just as easily be interpreted, many insist, as being fulfilled in the eternal heavenly kingship of Jesus Christ. Sadly, though, this is only possible when you excise the verse in question and isolate it from its proper context. Were it not for the verse following the promise about David's throne, then certainly, one might concede this perpetual kingdom was fulfilled in Christ. But what does the context provide us, without which "text without context" is error? Of this king in question, Nathan has God saying to David:

> When your days are fulfilled and you rest with your fathers, I'll raise up your descendant after you, who will come from your own body, and I'll establish his kingdom. He'll build a house for My name, and I'll establish the throne of his kingdom forever. I'll be his Father, and he'll be My son. When he does wrong, I'll discipline him with the rod of men and with the blows of the sons of men.[96]

Many are quick to point out here: "Look, this is clearly a descendant who comes from David's own body and whose throne will stand forever. What else can this be but the everlasting throne of the Lord Jesus Christ?"

And why do they say this, in spite of the verse that states: When he does wrong, I'll discipline him with the rod of men and with the blows of the sons of men? Why do they say this, in spite of the fact that God never had to discipline the sinless

---

95   *Psalm 89:34-37*

96   *Second Samuel 7:12-14*

Son of God, Jesus, with the hand of any man? Of course, they say it for the same reason Thomas Paine insisted that God failed to keep His promises in regard to the people of Israel. However, because they don't want to deny their faith in God, they're forced to find another way to dismiss what seems to be a lack of performance on God's part. So they spiritualize the kingship of David, because they too are aware of the traditional view of history that records the end of Judah's royal line when the Babylonian king blinded Zedekiah and killed his sons. But again, the only problem with that proposition is, the promise to David, of a perpetual earthly kingship, doesn't go away just because a traditional view of history doesn't satisfy the requirements of this promise.

That said, the answer to this mystery clearly requires a different solution. One thing is certain, though, when investigating the subject of God's promises, notwithstanding the objections of skeptics and critics, the acid test is still: What do you place your trust in, the promises of God or the traditions of man?

God Isn't a Man That He Lies

EVEN A heathen soothsayer like Balaam knew it was useless to argue with God. How ironic, then, that while many evangelical Christians have more in common with agnostics like Thomas Paine, the Scriptures have Balaam declaring:

> God isn't a man that He lies, or a son of man that He changes His mind. Does He speak and not act? Does He promise and not fulfill?"[97]

What's more, it should interest us to learn that while *The Bible* records just four prophetic utterances of Balaam—or oracles, as scholars call them—he had some very pertinent things to say in regard to our present inquiry. More importantly, what he said is all the more poignant considering these oracles weren't spoken by an Israelite prophet but, rather, a heathen soothsayer.

In Balaam, then, we have another example of a walking, talking paradox so commonplace in the scriptural record. And

---

97 *Numbers 23:19*

while this should force us to pay attention to what he said, all too often his prophetic wisdom is taken for granted. In light of the overall scheme of things depicted in this work, though, it shouldn't be difficult to push past such traditional blinders.

So, let's see what Balaam said, some of which has immediate application, while some of it will shed light on future aspects of our investigation. For the sake of cutting to the chase, let's condense Balaam's story as follows:

> Balak, son of Zippor, who was king of Moab at that time, summoned Balaam, son of Beor, who was at Pethor, near the Euphrates River, in his native land.
>
> And Balak said to Balaam, "A people have come out of Egypt; they cover the face of the land and have settled next to me. Now come and put a curse on these people, because they are too powerful for me. Perhaps then I'll be able to defeat them and drive them out of the land. For I know that whoever you bless is blessed, and whoever you curse is cursed..."
>
> Then Balaam took up a parable, and said, "Balak, the king of Moab, brought me from Aram, out of the mountains of the east, saying, 'Come, curse Jacob, and come, defy Israel.'
>
> "But how can I curse whom God hasn't cursed? Or how can I defy whom the Lord hasn't defied?
>
> "For from the hills I look upon him: See, the people dwell alone, and won't be reckoned among the nations.
>
> "Who can count the dust of Jacob, and the number of the fourth part of Israel?"[98]

How interesting is that? While theologians and scholars down through the ages have heatedly debated whether Balaam was rightly or wrongly included in the scriptural record, he somehow saw what few could've known at that time. What Balak could only see with the eyes in his head, Balaam saw with his inward eyes. Balak saw the mass of people invading his land, while Balaam, speaking in a day with neither printing press nor social media, had the foresight to echo the very words that God

---

98   Numbers 22:4-6; 23:7-10

intimately spoke to Abraham as recorded in *Genesis*: "Your descendants will be like the dust of the Earth."

And that's not all. Listen to what else Balaam said about the emerging new nation of Israel—in direct defiance of Balak's demands—just beginning to make its presence known to the inhabitants of Palestine:

> Look and see, I've received commandment to bless; and so He's blessed. I can't reverse it!
>
> He hasn't found iniquity in Jacob, neither has He seen perverseness in Israel. The Lord his God is with him, and the shout of a king is among them!
>
> God brought them out of Egypt; he has, as it were, the strength of a wild ox.
>
> Certainly there's no enchantment against Jacob, neither is there any divination against Israel. Speaking of this time one day, it will be said of Jacob and of Israel, "What has God wrought!"
>
> See, the people will rise up as a great lion, and lift up as a young lion; he won't lie down until he eats his prey, and drinks the blood of the slain...
>
> How lovely are your tents, oh Jacob, and your tabernacles, oh Israel! Like valleys they *spread out*, like gardens beside a river, like aloes planted by the Lord, like cedars beside the waters.
>
> He will pour the water out of his buckets, and his seed will be in many waters, and his king will be higher than Agag, and his kingdom will be exalted.
>
> God brought him forth out of Egypt; he has, as it were, the strength of a wild ox. He'll eat up the nations his enemies, and will break their bones, and pierce them through with his arrows.
>
> He couched, he lay down as a lion, and as a great lion; who shall stir him up? Blessed is he that blesses you, and cursed is he that curses you.[99]

Descendants like dust, revealed first to Abraham, and then, as we'll see in a moment, to his grandson Jacob, is here con-

---

99 *Numbers 23:20-24; 24:5-9*

firmed in the words of the most unlikely source we could expect. But notice several other key points that Balaam tunes in on. "The Lord his God is with him," said Balaam, "and the shout of the king is among them!" But not just any shout, because according to the meaning conveyed in the Hebrew, this shout is the shout of alarm, the shout of war! But fear not, oh Israel, according to Balaam nothing will deter them in battle—no enchantment, no divination. On this point, Scripture is clear.

However, what is unclear is the real reason for Balaam's repetition concerning Jacob's exodus from Egypt, when he describes their strength as being like both a wild ox and a lion, and that they'll eat up enemy nations, break their bones, pierce them with arrows, and drink their blood. Why do I say unclear?

I say that because most assume when Balaam twice said that God brought Jacob out of Egypt, followed by all they'd do afterwards through divine strength, he was repeating himself like many Hebrew poetic utterances repeat themselves. But I'd suggest that by insisting on this, one misses out on a vast portion of hidden meaning in the prophetic words of this heathen soothsayer. And mind you, these are words which have so far been proven genuine despite the skeptics and critics who insist God's word could never flow through such a one as Balaam.

His Seed Will Be in Many Waters

IN THIS CASE, when Balaam repeats himself about Jacob's exodus from Egypt, I believe we're not seeing a poetic repetition but, rather, a *prophetic* repetition. Which is just another way of saying that Balaam is actually describing, however unclear it was to him at the time, a dual event in God's plan of the ages. I'll explain this more fully down the line, but presently I can only hint at my complete explanation. Suffice it to say for now, my argument that Balaam was describing a dual event, hinges on the wording in the preceding passage, where Balaam said:

> How lovely are your tents, oh Jacob, and your tabernacles, oh Israel! Like valleys they *spread out*, like gardens beside a river, like aloes planted by the Lord, like cedars *beside the waters*.

He will pour *the water* out of his buckets, and his *seed* will be *in many waters*, and his king will be higher than Agag, and his kingdom will be exalted.[100]

And though I can't reveal the whole story yet, I can provide a clue as to what Balaam saw with his inward eyes. Proof of what he saw, once again, is revealed in the Hebrew words used here in Scripture. In this instance, we see Balaam speaking of the tents of Jacob "spreading out" like gardens beside a river and cedars "beside the waters," and the "seed" of Israel being "in many waters." In describing the tabernacles of Israel in this way, Balaam wasn't just echoing the same idea that describes the inexorable worldwide migration of the sons of Adam, Noah, and Abraham. He was also providing us with two reinforcing ideas important to this study of God's expanding Empire.

First, in his repeated references—to water, water, and more water—Balaam confirms, in no uncertain terms, how these migrations of God's people were to be uniquely facilitated via the waterways of the Earth. But consider this: When Moses led the Israelites forth from Egypt, apart from the Red Sea, by way of which bodies of water did they travel? According to every record of history I know of, they wandered through the Sinai Desert for forty years before getting to the Promised Land, which was itself only gifted with one river and two minor bodies of water—the Jordan River, the Sea of Galilee, and the Dead Sea.

Pardon me for stating the obvious, then, but traveling past—or through, as was the case with the Red Sea and the Jordan River—the aforementioned bodies of water hardly qualify as being "in many waters." So, for this portion of the prophecy to be as true as that which speaks of Jacob being brought forth from Egypt, then the route of any exodus from Egypt required a different route than the one Moses took. More on this alternate route will proceed in subsequent chapters, I assure you.

And second, by way of these verses, Balaam also used another word that's critically important to this study of the various migrations of God's people. The word is one that Balaam used when he spoke of the "seed" of Israel that "will be in many

---

100 *Numbers 24:5-7*

waters." That Hebrew word is *zera*, meaning not just "seed," in the sense of "children," or "descendants." According to *Strong's Exhaustive Concordance*, this word *zera* also speaks "especially of the seed of David as anointed to reign" and "as sitting on a throne." As it is written: "The Lord is a tower of salvation to His king, and He shows mercy to His anointed, to David and his *descendants* forevermore."[101] This is borne out by the fact that when Balaam spoke of these descendants, he didn't just speak of the descendants of Israel in general. If you notice, he said, "His seed will be in many waters, and his king will be higher than Agag, and his kingdom will be exalted."

The first thing we need to point out here is that this phrase "higher than Agag" is a common idiom of that day and age that spoke of the highest king in the land. We say the same thing about Egypt's pharaoh, which spoke of pharaoh, like Agag, as a synonym for king. As such, in a land of many kings who were reigning over many nations, the one who was said to be "higher than Agag" was being described as the highest king of them all.

What's more, this word *zera* carries with it a similar meaning from another Hebrew word, from which it's derived; that word is *zara*. It just so happens that the word *zara* provides us with another clue to solve the mystery of *who* and *where* to find this "other people" with whom God plans to make the original Israelites jealous and angry. That's because this word *zara* doesn't contain just the idea of sowing seeds locally, but it also carries the idea of a worldwide *scattering* of seeds, or descendants. We see this idea expressed in numerous biblical passages, such as:

> I will strengthen the House of Judah, and I will save the House of Joseph. I'll bring them back because I have compassion on them, and they'll be as though I had never rejected them, for I am the Lord their God, and I'll answer them.
>
> Though I *scattered* them among the nations, yet in faraway countries they'll remember Me, and with their children they'll live and return.[102]

---

101   *Second Samuel 22:51*

102   *Zechariah 10:6, 9*

What's more, in this root Hebrew word *zara*, which speaks of the scattering of Abraham's descendants, we have yet another clue to solve this great whodunit of the ages. Not to be missed in all this talk of royalty is something that's completely lost in any English translation of *The Bible*. This word *zara* just happens to describe more than the scattering of Israel's seed; it's also the name that was chosen at the birth of one of Judah's twin sons, Zarah, from the Hebrew word *zerach*, which means "dawning," or "radiance," as in, a "scattering of light." The psalmist had this very thing in mind when he wrote: "Light is *sown* for the righteous, and gladness for the upright in heart."[103]

In the first book of *The Bible*, we learn of the strange story surrounding the birth of this royal son of Judah, named Zarah, and his twin brother Pharez—a story that has incredible implications to this work, which has so much to do with the dividing, scattering, and uniting of God's people throughout history.

In the thirty-eighth chapter of *Genesis*, we read about the third son of Jacob, Judah, the man whom God deigned to father the royal lineage destined to rule and reign over the descendants of Israel for all time. Not only that, but it was also said that from Judah the long-awaited Messiah would one day come to save all Israel. So, as you can imagine, Satan, from that point onward, took special interest in this chosen man, and took every precaution to foul up God's purposes in his life.

As the story goes, Judah had three sons—Er, Onan, and Shelah—all of whom were in line to take up their father's regal mantle in due time. But when it came time for Er to raise children of his own, *The Bible* records that he refused, preferring to withhold his "seed" from his wife Tamar, no doubt hoping to avoid fathering any rivals to his impending throne. So records Scripture: "God killed Er because he was wicked in His sight."[104]

After that, Judah turned to his second-born son Onan and insisted he perform his duty as Er's brother, to provide children for the family and continue the royal lineage. But Onan resisted in the same way that Er had. As it is written:

---

103   Psalm 97:11

104   Genesis 38:7

Because Onan knew the child wouldn't be his, whenever he slept with his brother's wife, he spilled his semen on the ground to keep from providing offspring for his brother. What he did was wicked in the Lord's sight, so the Lord put him to death also.[105]

Then, Judah, fearing the same thing might happen to his last son Shelah, sent Tamar away to live with her father. And there she stayed, hoping, praying, pining, that one day Judah would do right by her, by uniting her with Shelah and thus remove her shame of being left childless.

But as time went by—so much so that by then Judah's wife had died—Judah still had yet to visit Tamar. Eventually, it became all too apparent to Tamar that unless she took matters into her own hands, she was doomed to a life of exile through no fault of her own.

At this point *The Bible* records a most dramatic turn of events. Instead of allowing herself to be passed over by her callous, paranoid father-in-law, Tamar sprang into action as soon as she heard that Judah was on his way to nearby Timnah to shear his sheep. Tamar then did something astonishing; she put away her widow's dress and covered herself with a seductive veil, in order to disguise her true identity. Then she cunningly placed herself along the road as Judah passed by. And thinking that no one would take notice of him, upon seeing the veiled Tamar, Judah approached her, assuming she was just another nameless, faceless prostitute.

Not realizing that she was his daughter-in-law, Judah went to her by the roadside and said, "Come now, let me sleep with you."

"And what will you give me to sleep with you?" Tamar asked.

"I'll send you a young goat from my flock," he said.

"Will you give me something as a pledge until you send it?" she asked.

He said, "What pledge should I give you?"

---

105   *Genesis 38:9*

"Your seal and its cord, and the staff in your hand," she answered. So he gave them to her and slept with her, and she became pregnant by him. After she left, she took off her veil and put on her widow's clothes again.

Meanwhile, Judah sent the young goat by his friend, the Adullamite, in order to get his pledge back from the woman, but he didn't find her. So he asked a man who lived there, "Where's the shrine prostitute who was beside the road at Enaim?"

"There were no shrine prostitutes here," he said.

So he went back to Judah, and said, "I didn't find her. Besides, a man who lived there said, 'There weren't any shrine prostitutes here.'"

Then Judah said, "Let her keep what she has, or we'll become a laughingstock. After all, I sent her this young goat, but you didn't find her."

About three months later, Judah was told, "Your daughter-in-law Tamar is guilty of prostitution, and as a result she's now pregnant."

Judah said, "Bring her out, and burn her to death!"

As she was being brought out, she sent a message to her father-in-law. "I'm pregnant by the man who owns these," she said. And she added, "See if you recognize whose seal and cord and staff these are."

Judah recognized them, and said, "She's more righteous than I, since I wouldn't give her to my son Shelah." And he never slept with her again.

When the time came for Tamar to give birth, there were twin boys in her womb. As she was giving birth, one of them put out his hand; so the midwife took a scarlet thread and tied it on his wrist, and said, "This one came out first." But when he drew back his hand, his brother came out, and she said, "So this is how you have broken out!" And he was named Pharez. Then his brother, who had the scarlet thread on his wrist, came out; and he was named Zarah.[106]

---

106 *Genesis 38:16-30*

What's in a Name

IT SHOULD be understood at this point that not only do biblical names reveal divine truths but also the very lives of individuals tell a tale just waiting to be unveiled by the discerning. We see this in the way the Apostle Paul saw how the lives of Abraham's sons revealed a hidden truth about God's contractual relationship with His people. Concerning Ishmael and Isaac, Paul said they were actually a metaphor for two ways of life, which is to say, one that led to slavery, while the other led to freedom.

> For it is written: Abraham had two sons, one by the slave woman and the other by the free woman. His son by the slave woman was born according to the flesh, but his son by the free woman was born according to the promise. These things serve as illustrations, for the women represent two covenants. One covenant is from Mount Sinai and bears children into slavery: This is Hagar. Now Hagar stands for Mount Sinai in Arabia and corresponds to the present-day Jerusalem, because she is in slavery with her children. But the Jerusalem above is free, and she is our mother…
>
> Now you, brothers, like Isaac, are children of promise… Therefore, we're not children of the slave woman, but of the free woman.[107]

Likewise, when Paul spoke of Jacob and Esau, he discerned a divine message in what those twin sons of Isaac represented, which is that, one was of the flesh, and one was of the promise.

> So the children of the flesh aren't God's children, but the children of the promise are regarded as His offspring. For this is what the promise stated: "At the appointed time I will return, and Sarah will have a son."
>
> Not only that, but Rebecca's children were also conceived by one man, our father Isaac. Yet before the twins were born or had done anything good or bad, in order that God's plan of election might stand, not by works but by Him Who calls, she was told, "The older will

---

107   *Galatians 4:22-26, 28, 31*

serve the younger."

So it is written: "Jacob I loved, but Esau I hated."[108]

In the same way, before the twin sons of Judah even had a chance to grow up and make their own mark on the world, their naming already conveyed an important lesson about God's control over history and His faithfulness to mankind. In the case of Zarah and Pharez, their names can be translated in various ways, all of which have important implications to this work, and which in turn lead us to a greater appreciation of the role played by these forebearers of every king and queen to be born of the House of Israel and the House of Judah.

Pharez can mean "breach," "breaker," "break out," "burst forth," "division," "disperse," "spread abroad," "rupture," and "blossom." Notice how, in addition to introducing new word meanings such as "breach," "breaker," and "break out," we see the connection this word has with previous words we've already discussed, such as "division," "disperse," and "spread abroad."

Zarah can mean "seed," "descendant," "scatter," "sow," "winnow," "disperse," "dawning," "radiance," and "sift." Notice how, in Zarah's case, in addition to conveying the meaning of "dawning" and "radiance," which is what we saw earlier with this word's connection with "light," we also see a clear over-lapping of meaning, in connection with previous words we've looked at, such as "scatter," "sow," and "disperse."

By way of what God intended to do, then, via the migratory drama of these regal twins, we catch a glimpse in their prophetic names: Zarah—in the "sowing" of light amongst all the nations of the world—and Pharez—the "break out" point from which those dispersed ones would venture forth with the blessing of Abraham.

Thus, the importance of the naming of these two royal brothers can never be overstated; however, before I can fully flesh out this idea, please remember our present line of inquiry: First, what evidence is there that as Abraham's descendants grow into many nations, they can't be contained where tradition has them living? Second, what evidence is there that wherever

---

108   *Romans 9:8-13*

they've gone, they'll be ruled over by a perpetual earthly dynasty of the line of David? Third, what evidence is there that these people are the same ones who Moses described as being "without understanding" and "not a people," of whom it was said that God would make fat and bloated Israel jealous and angry? And fourth, what evidence is there to connect this earthly kingdom with the nations that would one day flow into and become the future nation, out of many nations, called America?

So, if the verse in *Second Samuel*, speaking of a king of Israel, isn't referring to Jesus, and if traditional history has failed to locate the perpetual earthly kingship of Israel, then where should we look to find the fulfillment of these promises of God?

To which I'd reply, "Why not look to where we'll find evidence of God's faithfulness concerning the dust-like nature of Abraham's descendants who comprise the many nations?"

Which leads us to that other clue I spoke of earlier that we'd be dealing with in due time: There was something else that Nathan told David concerning the Lord's promises to him and his descendants. It's been written there for all to see, bearing witness to God's promise for millennia, yet it's so easily overlooked. Either that or like the tendency to spiritualize the earthly kingship of David, by insisting it's fulfilled in the heavenly kingship of Jesus, the verse in question is glossed over as well, by insisting it's speaking of Heaven rather than of Earth. Oddly enough, though, when we resist the urge to spiritualize these words, we find ourselves confronting the very clues we need to answer the questions we keep asking. Clues that actually lead us to discovering where these dust-like descendants are inhabiting a land of many nations.

CHAPTER ELEVEN

WHEN NEW WINE BREAKS FORTH

Now then, you're to tell My servant David, this is what the Lord of Hosts says: "I'll provide a place for My people Israel and will plant them so they may live in a place of their own and be disturbed no more. No longer will the sons of wickedness oppress them as they did at the beginning and have done since the day I appointed judges over My people Israel. I'll give you rest from all your enemies." (Second Samuel 7:10-11)

To Make Earth More Like Heaven

BY LOOKING to the prayer Jesus taught His disciples, we're sure to engage our investigation on the level that's necessary to discern all things biblical. Of course, I say this assuming we remember how I'm suggesting we look at the Disciples' Prayer. While others gloss over its implications, we embrace them. When we pray with the disciples, "Father, Your will be done, on Earth as it is in Heaven," we accept God's injunction to use us to make Earth more like Heaven, instead of trying to coerce God to remove us from this life and send us straight into the afterlife.

After all, isn't that what makes Judaism and Christianity different from all other world religions? As it is written:

The Earth is the Lord's and all its fullness—the world and all who live in it.[109]

While other religions seek to escape this veil of tears, or to transcend the wheel of life, or to mortify the flesh, the biblical God redeems what others never hope to redeem. That's why it's so sad to watch as Christians succumb to this same tendency to abhor this earthly life, as though it were unrecoverable and only good for the trash heap.

In this confused effort, we're doubtlessly besieged by so many paradoxes of Scripture. But in every case, we're really succumbing to the inconsistencies of interpretation rather than to the paradoxes themselves, which can be resolved if we're willing to look at the whole book of God. Then we'd find we're to mortify the "deeds" of the flesh, not the flesh itself. We're to reckon our "old selves" as dead in Christ, not our "new selves" that are alive in Christ, in the here and now.

Again, as much biblical evidence as there is to believe our goal is to die and go to Heaven, there's even more evidence to reveal Christ's resurrection and the Day of Pentecost inaugurated a new era of human existence. With this new era, the Earth can, in anticipation of the emancipation of God's children, begin to experience a new creation of its own, one person at a time, just as the saints are becoming new creations in Christ, on Earth as it is in Heaven.

What's more, this appreciation of God's affinity to this earthly existence is also how Christianity and Judaism differ from other religions in their approach to history itself. Both biblical faiths grow out of specific historical events that can be pointed to with a fair amount of certainty. Not so with other world religions, be they religious or mythological histories. While chronologists might disagree as to the exact date of the exodus from Egypt or the resurrection of Christ, no similar attempts are offered to locate in time the founding of Mount Olympus by the gods of Greece or of the death and resurrection of Tammuz of Babylonia.

One thing is certain, though: These turning points in bib-

---

109   *Psalm 24:1*

lical history can be localized, historically speaking. In the case of the Exodus, history records an abrupt vacuum of power in Egyptian history at the same time as the "alleged" destruction of Pharaoh's entire army. From that point onward, the nation of escaped Israelites were suddenly able to wander about the Sinai Peninsula for forty years with no record of their ever being attacked by said army again.

Similarly, while historians debate the reality of the "alleged" resurrection of Christ, history records a complete turnabout in the lives of Christ's disciples. Following the crucifixion, they all cowered in their homes for fear of the Jewish leaders, then suddenly, almost overnight, they all became fearless witnesses to the resurrection; willingly and without hesitation, they all endured withering persecution, and one by one, in far flung corners of the world, they accepted martyrdom rather than recant their testimony.

In short, while other world religions are entirely rooted in philosophy and ethics, the biblical religions, from old to new, uniquely embrace a historical perspective without reservation or apology.

How odd, then, when those of so staunchly a historical mindset insist a certain prophecy could not have been fulfilled in "physical" terms therefore it must have been fulfilled in "spiritual" terms. Again, I say: How does that even make sense? But, sadly, such is the thought process Jesus must have had in mind when He taught His disciples—and us—to enlist God's help to make Earth more like Heaven with each passing prayer.

Or else what would be the point in Jesus giving His disciples the keys of the Kingdom of Heaven? Why tell them to bind or loose on Earth what would then be bound or loosed in Heaven? Why tell them that if two or three on Earth agree about anything, it would be done for them by the Father in Heaven? Are we to assume that whenever God doesn't seem to answer the prayers of those who invoke these words of Christ, that their prayers were answered spiritually speaking? Persist in that sort of logic, in the face of rampant doubt and skepticism, and we'll soon be up to our ears in Thomas Paines. It's because of such spiritualizing efforts that mankind has ceased to even search out

God's historical record of performance in regard to His promises to His people.

That's because when we spiritualize the fulfillment of God's promises to Abraham, we wind up doing the opposite of what the Church should be doing, which is to articulate God's faithfulness to a dying world in the here and now. The end result: We create a mindset that all but avoids studying prophecy lest we stumble onto any inconsistencies that must be dismissed in the name of avoiding anything that contradicts our pet theory of Scripture.

Case in point are these promises to King David that are crucial to a proper understanding of God's faithfulness to Abraham, Sarah, and their descendants. Not only will *kings* come from them, but these kings will also constitute a *perpetual kingship*, with an *earthly throne* lasting throughout all time. Fail to acknowledge that *all three* conditions are outlined in *The Bible*, fail to acknowledge that *all three* promises of God must be fulfilled, and you too will find yourself jumping on the bandwagon of Christian spiritualizers of biblical prophecy.

Let's revisit those promises, then, not just of a perpetual kingship of David's descendants but of an earthly place where those kings and queens are to rule and reign. Said God to Nathan:

> Now then, you're to tell My servant David, this is what the Lord of Hosts says: "I'll provide a place for My people Israel and will plant them so they may live in a place of their own and be disturbed no more. No longer will the sons of wickedness oppress them as they did at the beginning and have done since the day I appointed judges over My people Israel. I'll give you rest from all your enemies…
>
> "I'll personally establish a house for you. And when your days are fulfilled and you rest with your fathers, I'll raise up your descendant after you, who will come from your own body, and I'll establish his kingdom. He'll build a house for My name, and I'll establish the throne of his kingdom forever. I'll be his Father, and he'll be My son. When he does wrong, I'll discipline him with

the rod of men and with the blows of the sons of men.

"But My loving devotion will never be removed from him as I removed it from Saul, whom I moved out of your way. Your house and kingdom will endure forever before Me, and your throne will be established forever."[110]

Their King Will Pass Through

NOW IN TRYING to locate where God would provide a place for David's royal lineage to rule over His people Israel, we have to first address the traditional view that the land given to them only involved Palestine, or the so-called "Promised Land," as Scripture calls it. But if that were true, then even God would have a hard time keeping His promise to Abraham. Why? Because if Abraham's descendants did become as numerous as the dust of the Earth, then they'd never be able to fit into the geographical area of Palestine, which amounts to less than 7,000 square miles.

Fortunately for us, though, God's word does offer a solution to this problem. In this instance, we discover that the key to unlocking this mystery is revealed in something that God told Abraham's grandson Jacob, even before he was renamed Israel.

Most everyone who's ever read *The Bible* remembers the scene in which this reiteration of God's promise took place. It's the one where the young patriarch Jacob is fleeing his murderous brother Esau who is hunting him down after he's tricked him out of his family birthright yet again. Sometime during the night, Jacob dreamt of a great celestial stairway, connecting Heaven and Earth, with the angels of God ascending and descending this stairway. We know it today as Jacob's Ladder; but what most people overlook about this dream is what the Lord told Jacob from that ladder:

And there at the top, the Lord was standing and saying, "I am the Lord, the God of your fathers, Abraham and Isaac. I'll give you and your descendants the land on which you now lie. Your descendants will be like the

---

dust of the Earth, and you'll *spread out* to the west and east and north and south. All the families of the Earth will be blessed through you and your offspring."[111]

Of course, it's not surprising that most people overlook the implications of God's promise to Jacob, because rarely if ever is the story of Abraham and his children viewed in the context of the larger drama of God compelling Adam's descendants to fill the whole Earth.

Notice in this verse, God didn't just repeat the promise He first gave to Abraham. He also added that in their descendants fulfilling this promise to become like dust, it included their having to "spread out" in every direction so that all the families of the Earth could be blessed. In this, we encounter another Hebrew word, *parats*, that's similar to what we saw in the case of Noah and his family. There we saw how God ordered Noah and his sons to "spread out" across the world; there the word was *parad*, which spoke of both "spreading out" and "dividing."

In the case of Jacob, who as it should be remembered was renamed Israel, the Scriptures now employ a similar word but with an added dimension. The Hebrew word for "spreading out" here, *parats*, not only speaks of God's directive to Jacob and his children to expand their population, but it also speaks of a "breaking out" and a "breaking forth," as in, when new wine breaks forth from old wineskins. What's more, we'll soon see how this word *parats* provides the key to unlocking the mystery of God's promise that Abraham's offspring will bless all the families of the Earth.

To begin with, in this word *parats*, we see that the land of Palestine will undoubtedly belong to the descendants of Abraham. Of this all history will confirm as a witness to God's faithfulness to Israel. However, this land—of less than 7,000 square miles—won't be the only land involved in this blessing that's destined to impact the whole world.

What this verse is really saying, when we understand the implications of this word *parats*, is that Palestine is merely the cradle for a much larger movement as it pertains to God's ex-

---

111 Genesis 28:13-14

panding Empire. That's because while Abraham's family began in earnest there, it could by no means accommodate a dust-like people whose destiny was to "break forth" like new wine from its original container en route to blessing all humanity.

And just in case you think I'm being overly dramatic with my declaration, let me provide just a taste of why I believe this to be true. Not only is this word *parats*, and its derivatives, used throughout Scripture to describe this "spreading out" and "breaking forth," but *parats* is also the root word for the name of the twin son of Judah, Pharez, of which came the royal line of David, from which Jesus of Nazareth would one day be born. You should recall the twin sons of Judah—Zarah and Pharez— because we introduced them in the last chapter, where I also mentioned that just as God illustrated His divine wisdom by way of the lives of previous brothers, like Ishmael and Isaac, and Jacob and Esau, the names of these twin sons of Judah also reveal an important truth.

In the case of Zarah, his name typified the way that not only were the descendants of Israel to be "scattered" and "sown as light" amongst the nations of the world but, more specifically, how this scattering pertained to the royal line of Judah as well. Now here we are discovering yet another way that the names of the twin sons of Judah reveal a hidden truth that will lead us to a completely unexpected thing. Whereas Zarah and his descendants were to be "scattered as light," Pharez and his descendants provide the clue as to where that "scattering" began, and to where that "scattering" went.

That's because, as it turns out, the root word for Pharez is another of those words that's embedded in numerous biblical verses, in the same way as several other words I've already cited, like *parad*, *parar*, *palag*, and *puwts*. In this case, it's the same word the prophet Micah used when he wrote:

I will surely gather all of you, oh Jacob; I'll collect the remnant of Israel. I'll bring them together like sheep in a pen, like a flock in the midst of its pasture—a noisy throng. One who *breaks open* the way will go up before them; they'll *break through* the gate, and go out by it.

Their king will pass through before them, the Lord as their leader.[112]

In this case, when Micah spoke of one who "breaks open" the way, and those who "break through" the gate, he used a derivative of this Hebrew word *parats*. Not only does this word provide the key to unlocking the mystery of how Abraham's descendants will bless all humanity, but it also helps to explain how Jesus Christ accomplished His messianic work in a completely unexpected way. In short, this verse speaks of an ancient messianic personage—of the royal line of Judah, as we'll later see from sacred history—who typifies Christ, as one "who breaks open the way and passes through" before "the people" who, in turn, follow this king, in "breaking through the gate and going out by it."

This verse, I submit, provides us with the foundational Scripture upon which rests my entire argument in this work. It is the key that unlocks the door that leads us to where God destined the perpetual earthly kingship of David to rule and reign. It explains how God provided a place for His people Israel, to plant them so they'd live in a place of their own and be disturbed no more. It explains the role played by Judah's twin sons—Zarah and Pharez—in the transplanting effort of God's people. And it explains how technology aided in this transplanting effort, as well as how technology aided the birth, growth, and progress of the land that would one day be called America.

But before I explain how the word *parats*, and the verse in *Micah*, and the twin sons of Judah provide all this, I'll first need to introduce an important ingredient into the mix. I'll need to introduce a man you all know. But, in this instance, I'll introduce not just the man but also the mission he personally gave to his followers. It's a mission that everyone who's ever read *The Bible* has heard about, yet it's a mission that has for too long been shrouded in mystery. Why?

Well, for one thing, it's because the God of Set Times fore-ordained a very specific time frame to elapse before the true meaning of this mission would be fully made known to human-

---

ity. It's also been shrouded in mystery because the traditions of mankind are so hard to shake once they've taken hold with such strength. And finally, this mystery is difficult to penetrate because even though God's set time to reveal this knowledge has arrived, it requires a mindset that's open to the idea that God's hidden hand is involved in every aspect of human history.

It is for just such a mindset, then, that proof of God's fingerprints, indelibly stamped throughout history, has been patiently waiting to be discovered.

Chapter Twelve

A NATION THAT WILL BEAR FRUIT

Then Jesus said, "Haven't you ever read in the Scriptures? The stone the builders rejected has become the cornerstone. This is from the Lord, and it's marvelous in our eyes. So I tell you, the Kingdom of God will be taken from you and given to a nation that will bear fruit. He who falls on this stone will be broken to pieces, but he on whom it falls will be crushed." (Matthew 21:42-44)

Another Piece of the Puzzle

ONE DAY, Jesus and His disciples approached Jerusalem, where they arrived at the Mount of Olives. Jesus then made a strange request of the disciples. "Go into the village up ahead, and there you'll find a donkey with her colt next to her. Untie them, and bring them to Me. If anyone questions you, tell them the Lord needs them, and He'll return them shortly." This, the Apostle Matthew tells us, was done to fulfill the words spoken by the prophet:

Say to the daughter of Zion, "See, your King comes to you, gentle and riding on a donkey—on a colt, the foal of a donkey."[113]

---

113 *Zechariah 9:9*

So the disciples went and did as Jesus had directed them. They brought the donkey and the colt, and laid their cloaks on them, and Jesus sat upon the colt.

A massive crowd spread their cloaks on the road, while others cut branches from the trees, and spread them before Him.

The crowds that went ahead of Jesus, and those who followed, were shouting: "Hosanna to the Son of David!" "Blessed is He Who comes in the name of the Lord!" "Hosanna in the highest!"

When Jesus had entered Jerusalem, the whole city was in an uproar, and someone asked, "Who is this?"

And another replied, "This is Jesus, the prophet from Nazareth, in Galilee."

Later that day, Jesus entered the temple courts and drove out all who were buying and selling there. He overturned the tables of the money changers and the seats of those selling doves. And He yelled at them, "It is written: My house will be called a house of prayer![114] But you've turned it into a den of thieves!"

Then, the blind and the lame began to come to Jesus at the Temple, and He healed them. But the chief priests and scribes grew angry when they saw the wonders He was performing and because the children were shouting in the temple courts, "Hosanna to the Son of David!"

"Do you hear what these children are saying?" one of the scribes asked Jesus.

"Yes, I do," He answered. "Haven't you ever read the Scripture? Out of the mouths of babes, You've ordained praise."[115]

Then Jesus left them and went out of the city to Bethany, where He spent the night.

In the morning, as Jesus was returning to the city, He was hungry. Seeing a fig tree by the road, He went up to it but found nothing on it except leaves. "May you never bear fruit again!" He said, and immediately the tree withered.

When Jesus returned to the temple courts and began to teach, the chief priests and elders came up to Him. A chief priest asked, "By what authority are You doing these things?"

---

114   Jeremiah 7:11

115   Psalm 8:2

And Jesus replied, "I'll also ask you a question, and if you answer Me, I'll tell you by what authority I'm doing these things. Fair enough?"

The priests and elders exchanged a nervous look, and one by one, they all nodded to each other, then they turned to Jesus. One of the priests nodded, and said, "Agreed."

Said Jesus, "What was the source of John's baptism? Was it from Heaven or from men?"

Turning to one another again, the priests and elders deliberated amongst themselves. One of the elders said in hushed tones, "If we say, 'From Heaven,' He'll ask, 'Then why didn't you believe him?' But if we say, 'From men,' there's no telling how the people might react, because they all think John is a prophet."

So they turned back toward Jesus, and one of the priests answered solemnly, "We don't know."

And Jesus replied, "Then neither will I tell you by what authority I do these things." And turning to the crowd there, Jesus continued. "So tell me: What do you think? There was a man who had two sons. He went to the first one and said, 'Son, go and work today in the vineyard.'

"And the son replied, 'I won't.' But later, he changed his mind and went.

"Then the man went to his second son, and told him the same thing. 'I will, sir,' he said. But that son didn't go. Which of these two sons did what his father wanted?"

One of the chief priests said confidently, "Naturally, the first one."

Jesus said to them, "That's right; and that's why tax collectors and prostitutes are entering the Kingdom of God before you. Because John came to you in a righteous way but still you didn't believe him, but the tax collectors and the prostitutes did. And even after you saw this, it still never entered your minds to repent and believe him.

"So listen, all of you, to another parable: There was a landowner who planted a vineyard. He put a wall around it, dug a winepress in it, and built a tower. Then he rented it out to some tenants and went away on a journey.

"When harvest time drew near, he sent his servants to the tenants to collect his share of the fruit. But the tenants seized his servants. They beat one, stoned another, and killed a third.

"Again, he sent other servants, more than the first group. But the tenants did the same to them.

"Finally, he sent his son to them. 'They'll respect my son,' the landowner said.

"But when the tenants saw the son, they said to one another, 'This is the heir. Come, let's kill him and take his inheritance.' Then they seized the son, thrust him out of the vineyard, and killed him.

"So, when the owner of the vineyard returns, what will he do to those tenants?"

Instantly, an elder of the people declared, "Naturally, he'll bring those wretches to a miserable end, and then he'll rent out the vineyard to other tenants who will give him his rightful share of the fruit at harvest time."

Then Jesus said, "Haven't you ever read in the Scriptures? The stone the builders rejected has become the cornerstone. This is from the Lord, and it's marvelous in our eyes.[116]

"So I tell you, the Kingdom of God will be taken from you and given to a nation that will bear fruit. He who falls on this stone will be broken to pieces, but he on whom it falls will be crushed."

And when Jesus concluded His parable, it occurred to the chief priests and Pharisees that He'd been speaking about them all along. And although they were very anxious to arrest Him, they were afraid of the crowds, because the people believed He was a prophet.[117]

The preceding events were recorded for all time, courtesy of the Apostle Matthew, in the twenty-first chapter of his gospel. Thanks to Matthew's keen sense of narrative, we have another piece of the puzzle we're assembling. It's time now to take these words of Jesus, and coordinate them with those that we've gathered to this point.

---

116 *Psalm 118:22–23*

117 *Matthew 21*

Heaven Only Knows

SO FAR, we've been looking to connect a series of ideas to determine where God had in mind when he inspired Nathan to tell David that a place was being prepared for the people of Israel. For anyone tempted to say this place was the Promised Land, please remember that David was already well established in Palestine when Nathan spoke of this transplanting effort.

This new place, however, would have several distinguishing features that make it clear Nathan couldn't possibly have been speaking of Palestine. That's because unlike Palestine, which had been occupied by seven hostile, heathen nations, this new place is described as being all their own, and where they wouldn't be disturbed or oppressed by the sons of wickedness, as they had been since their days in Canaan. And this, mind you, is in addition to what we've already discussed, which is that Palestine was somewhere that, because the Israelites were to become like the dust of the Earth, would never be able to contain them all.

Now here we are coming to grips with Matthew's narrative, which presents us with some much-needed information in solving this mystery. Not only does it demonstrate that Nathan's prophecy wasn't some random sidebar of biblical history, but it also provides us with an overarching view of why God removed His people from Palestine and transplanted them elsewhere.

What's more, it's important to see all this within the larger context of God's plan for humanity to spread out across the globe, in spite of every attempt of the devil to thwart that movement. We saw this tug of war in Noah's day when his sons resisted the divine call to disperse into all the Earth. We saw it after the Exodus when the Israelites preferred slavery in Egypt to marching in search of the Promised Land. So what was God's word to them in that day, when the Israelites failed to rise to the occasion, even after all the miracles they'd seen by the hand of Moses?

> You ignored the Rock Who brought you forth; you forgot the God Who gave you birth. When the Lord saw this, He rejected them; provoked to anger by His sons and daughters, He said: "I will hide My face from them.

I'll see what their end will be. For they're a perverse generation—children of unfaithfulness. They've provoked My jealousy by that which is not God; they've enraged Me with their worthless idols. So I'll make them jealous by those who are not a people; I'll make them angry by a nation without understanding."[118]

Then, just as Moses had spoken these words before the Israelites entered the Promised Land under the leadership of Joshua, Jesus spoke of a similar consequence in the lives of the Jewish nation in His day if they failed to live up to God's expectation for them. In the case of Jesus, they were to embrace Him as their Messiah and take upon themselves what He only later commissioned His disciples.

Heaven only knows, though, if the Jewish nation as a whole had accepted the lordship of the Man Who insisted that—as God's chosen nation—they weren't to lord over other nations as world conquerors, as Judas and Barabbas hoped to do. Rather, they were to be a light for the nations, to serve them, not to be served by them. But in demanding that Jesus conform to their expectations of lordship, they provoked the Lord of Creation. Just as they'd done in Moses' day, they did in Jesus' day as well, and in their rejection of the son of the master of the vineyard, they elicited a similar judgment. First Jesus, finding a fig tree without fruit—as a type of the Jewish nation in Palestine— cursed it and made it wither, never to bear fruit again. Then said Jesus to the priests and Pharisees who despised Him so much:

So I tell you, the Kingdom of God will be taken from you and given to a nation that will bear fruit.[119]

From Adam, to Noah, to Moses, to Nathan, to Jesus, we see a clear pattern—a divine blueprint, if you will. In each phase of the spreading outward of God's people into every corner of the globe, they're being told the same thing: God is giving you a place to begin anew, to do what the last group failed to do—to not only be fruitful, physically speaking, but to also be fruitful,

---

118   *Deuteronomy 38:18-21*

119   *Matthew 21:43*

spiritually speaking. In short, if you rise to the occasion through faith and sacrifice, then all will be well with you. But rest assured, God always has a backup plan should you fail. He's prepared another place beyond the borders of the old place, for the sake of another people outside the purview of the old people, where maybe they'll get it right the next time.

And just in case anyone think that I'm making an unwarranted connection between the physical and spiritual nature of God's injunction to "be fruitful," I'd like to point out that the scriptural record does confirm this connection. In this instance, there just happens to be another correlation of Hebrew words that Scripture employs in describing this divine blueprint, that is, in this interplay between God's commission of "fruitfulness" and His need to "divide" and "scatter" those who fail to live up to this commission. Just as there is an unmistakable continuity in the Hebrew words describing these divinely ordained "dividing" and "scattering" events, there is a similar continuity in regard to God's command to be "fruitful." Whereas words like *parad* and *parats* are used to describe God's "dividing" and "scattering," it turns out that whenever God told His people to be "fruitful," the Scriptures always employed another Hebrew word with a similar root meaning, which is to say, *parah*. In other words, whenever God told the next recipients of His commission to *parah*, or to "be fruitful," God eventually had to *parad* or *parats* them, or to "divide" and "scatter" them, to ensure it happened.

As such, God's original intention in telling humanity to be fruitful has never been a simple matter of physical plentifulness as one might assume in the natural. Rather, God's true purpose in the call of Abraham or the scattering of Israel, to be fruitful and multiply, was always intended to create a plentitude of people, which would constitute national Israel, from which a lesser group of individuals would emerge, which would in turn constitute spiritual Israel.

Couched in Ambiguity

SO HAVING established *why* God prepared another place for His people, we continue with what we've also been asking: *Who* might those people be? And *where* might that place be? At this point in our quest, I feel it's necessary to mention something else that's overlooked in studies of this nature. In many ways, it's like that classic dilemma: Which comes first, the chicken or the egg? In this case, I believe there's something even more important than the *why*, the *who*, or the *where*. And that is the question of *if*. What do I mean by that?

Well, consider what we're dealing with when we try to prove whether or not "this" place or people are the "right" place or people. While we confidently claim to have evidence for *the* "this" or *the* "right," whether historical, archeological, or etymological, in the end, what we really have amounts to nothing more than "my word against yours." After all, we're not trying to prove something in the same way we prove who robbed whom or who murdered whom.

That's because God's way of delivering on His promises always involves His conveying promises that are purposefully couched in ambiguity and paradox. Therefore, before we set out to determine the historical fulfillment of any promise of God, it behooves us to first establish an approach that accounts for this ambiguous nature of the evidence.

With that in mind, I believe that before we look any further concerning the *who* and the *where* of this place and these people, we need to ask *if* Jesus Himself revealed anything more than what Moses and Nathan said about all this. In short, before we analyze the historical data to verify—say, for example—whether or not Jesus rose from the grave, we first need to determine *if* Jesus made claims about His resurrection prior to that event. After all, what point is there in trying to verify whether a given event occurred if no one ever predicted that event would occur?

Similarly, before we investigate the historical evidence for the relocation of anyone among the tribes of Israel, we should first confirm if Jesus Himself ever claimed that God intended to relocate Israel to some unknown land other than Palestine.

Now, in this attempt to invoke the claim of Jesus to validate our quest, we should also take note of something else. Ask yourself: If the resurrection of Christ is the foundational tenant of Christianity, then shouldn't we expect to see more references to it, in the words of the prophets, than we've seen concerning "another place" and "another people"?

I mean, God certainly could've made the resurrection of Christ clearer in His dramas of *The Old Testament*, which is to say, He could have if He wanted to make it clearer. Sure, He had Jonah survive for three days and nights in the belly of the whale; and yes, He had Abraham offer up his son Isaac as a burnt offering. But typically, the prophecies of Christ's death and resurrection are so obscure they could only be understood after the fact, and then only when one literally read between the lines of Scripture, as when the Apostle Peter did, in quoting King David anew, when he said:

> Men and brothers, let me speak freely to you of the patriarch David, that he's both dead and buried, and his tomb is with us to this day. Therefore, being a prophet, and knowing that God had sworn an oath to him, that of the fruit of his body according to the flesh, He would raise up the Christ to sit on his throne, he, foreseeing this, spoke concerning the resurrection of the Christ, that His soul was not left in Hades, nor did His flesh see corruption. This Jesus, God raised up, of which we're all witnesses.[120]

Then compare the scarce evidence for Christ's resurrection with that of the abundant evidence for the punishment of Israel, their subsequent relocation, and ultimate restoration.

Now, again, this doesn't mean God intends to entirely spell out such mysteries in His word simply for the sake of critics or skeptics. It just means that considering this abundance of evidence, the last thing people who are trying to undermine our investigation should be saying is there's no smoking gun to be found when looking for such evidence.

And just where is the biggest smoking gun of all, concerning the *who* and the *where*, in regard to the mystery of this "other place" and "other people"? Of course it's Jesus Himself, Who didn't just say the Kingdom of God would be taken from "the tenants who killed the landowner's son," and given to "a nation that will bear fruit." He also filled in more details to solve this

---

120   Acts 2:29-32

mystery, when He told the disciples who would be carrying out this mission of transplanting the Kingdom of God. In fact, Matthew had Jesus twice telling us who'd be doing the job.

Now, as I've said, the most important thing about this isn't so much that Jesus revealed the *who* and the *where* of this mission, because as usual the specifics of their identity and location will always be couched in ambiguity by virtue of how God designs His revelation. Therefore, the real importance of Jesus giving us this double-barreled revelation is that in doing so, He's provided us with the *if*. And by that I mean, *if* Jesus never said what He said, then there'd be absolutely no point in looking for the *who* and the *where*. But *if* He did say what He said—and He most certainly did say it—then suddenly the integrity of God's word is at stake, and a line has been drawn in the sand. Not just by the prophets of old who spoke of this mystery, not just by Moses, or by Nathan, or by the others we'll turn to in subsequent chapters, but also by Jesus Christ Himself.

Despite the decades of scholarship, then, attempting to prove one's case about this "other people" and that "other place," the fact is, *if* Jesus Himself revealed whose job it was to go to those people and to that place, then we have just two choices before us. Either we remove those parts from *The Bible*, like Thomas Jefferson did whenever he confronted something he found objectionable, or we admit that a people other than the original recipients of God's Kingdom exist, and that a place other than Palestine exists as well. In short, until we agree that Jesus confirmed the *if*, we'll never even be able to take the first step toward agreeing on the *who* and the *where*.

So, what did Jesus tell His disciples concerning these other people in another place? How are they connected to the idea that the Kingdom of God would be given to a nation that would bear fruit? Who did Jesus say would be given the responsibility of transplanting God's Kingdom? Is there any connection between this transplanted Kingdom, Daniel's Stone Kingdom, and the nation that Moses said would make Israel jealous and angry? And finally, if this connection can be found, how does it demonstrate a historical link between Israel of old and America today?

CHAPTER THIRTEEN

SENT ONLY TO THE LOST SHEEP

> *Leaving that place, Jesus withdrew to the district of Tyre and Sidon. And a Canaanite woman from that region came to Him, crying out, "Lord, Son of David, have mercy on me! My daughter is miserably possessed by a demon." But Jesus didn't answer her, so one of His disciples came and urged Him, "Send her away, because she keeps calling for us." He answered, "I was sent only to the lost sheep of the House of Israel." (Matthew 15:21-24)*

The People of His Choice

CONCERNING the question of *who* Moses, Nathan, and Daniel spoke of and *where* they are located, the Apostle Matthew adds a critical piece to the puzzle, in which God reveals a consistent pattern of doing the same thing throughout history. What we see in this, of course, goes back to God's way of ensuring the sons of Noah carry out His plan of spreading out across the Earth. Whether they cooperate willingly or unwillingly doesn't concern or deter Him in the least.

Now, in saying this, I'm not trying to make it sound as if God is callously, dispassionately moving people about like so many chess pieces. Far from it, in fact. Clearly, God has our greater good in mind, to which we as a rebellious and reckless people are often oblivious. That's the reason I'm trying so hard throughout this work to not simply chronicle the *who* and the *where* of this story but also the *why*. Because only by becoming aware of this pattern of God's scattering effort do we begin to see a side of God's character that's usually overlooked when we consider His judgments, which from our limited perspective sometimes appear harsh and cruel.

All too often, in response to critics and skeptics, we're convinced God is being vindictive in the divine judgments we see throughout biblical history. We're shocked and dumbfounded by the fire and brimstone that rained down on Sodom and Gomorrah, or the shattering judgments that landed on the kingdoms of Israel and Judah, when they were carried into captivity by Assyria and Babylon. But upon careful review of these events, in the context of the pattern of scattering and relocating, we might possibly see "through the looking glass," as it were, and see how God uniquely transcends our merely human view of things.

To us, death and disease are the greatest enemies we can know as finite creatures who are so susceptible to these stark horrors. But to God, Who understands our habit of taking His gifts for granted, these twin enemies of humanity work toward far different goals from His perspective. Critics and skeptics, hoping to capitalize on this evidence in their war against a biblical faith, insist death and disease prove that God either doesn't exist or doesn't care. But in fact, if God hadn't allowed death and disease to overtake humanity, after Adam and Eve ate from the Tree of Knowledge, God's promises of eternal life and physical healing would've proved utterly meaningless.

So, when we see beyond the surface view of the forced migrations of God's people, from age to age, we begin to see in these scattering efforts the actions of a parent who'd prefer we didn't have to learn the hard way about what we're told about sin and error. But if the people of His choice rebel and go their own way, as they so often insist on doing, God knows exactly how to effect the change He's looking for. He gets it done by invoking this timeless pattern: God first bestows His blessings on a people of His choosing. After that, the people reach the point where they take those blessings for granted, followed by their outright abuse of them. And finally, God allows the consequences of their own actions to trigger yet another scattering of said chosen people.

Like a Great Director

IN THE DAYS of Jesus, when the House of Judah could have accepted their true king, they rejected Him just as those wilderness wanderers did in Moses' day. But like a Great Director of a divine drama, God orchestrated every event to work His will regarding the number of the Children of Israel. That's because, unlike many a dispassionate director of human drama, God is passionately invested in the plight of His people, rebellious though they often are.

Jesus, likewise, was no less passionate about the sheep of His Father's pasture. When He could've lashed out at those who rejected Him, Jesus openly grieved. He wept bitterly over Jerusalem because He knew what was about to overtake them as the consequence of their disobedience. The Apostle Matthew described Jesus as crying out:

> Oh, Jerusalem, Jerusalem, you kill the prophets, and stone those sent to you. How often have I longed to gather your children together, as a hen gathers her chicks under her wings, but you were unwilling! Look, your house is left to you desolate. For I tell you, you won't see Me again until you say, "Blessed is He who comes in the name of the Lord."[121]

So does that mean Jesus was rejected by all the children of Jacob? Well, it certainly seems that way if we believe the traditional view of biblical history. But again, I'd like to introduce yet another of those glaring inconsistencies in Scripture that only seems like an inconsistency when we fail to push beyond the fact that we're really dealing with another paradox. That's because according to Jesus, His mission didn't involve just the House of Judah, and fortunately, we have Matthew to thank for that double-barreled declaration of which I spoke earlier.

In *The Gospel of Matthew*, we find this unique take on our tra-

---

ditional view of Jesus' mission. As so often happens, it's another of those famous pronouncements where people familiar with *The Bible* already know about what Jesus said, but never do they fully appreciate the implications of said pronouncements. It's just like when Christians and Jews alike have heard, again and again, that Abraham's descendants were to one day be counted as the dust of the Earth. Yet for some inexplicable reason, they never seem bothered that they can't locate these dust-like descendants where they're supposed to be located, so they simply repress the whole matter and hope nobody brings up the subject.

Similarly, when we confront what Jesus tells us next, please keep in mind we're dealing with the same human tendency that allows us to balance two contradictory statements in our brain without ever being concerned they're mutually exclusive ideas that can never co-exist with one another. Let's look at what I'm talking about.

Now that we've established there's no point in looking for the *who* or the *where* in our present mystery unless we know *if* Jesus Himself warranted such an investigation, we'll turn next to the Lord's statement that "the Kingdom of God will be taken from you"—that is, from those to whom it was originally offered—"and given to a nation that will bear fruit." Here I'm suggesting that this fruitful nation speaks of the same people of whom Jesus refers elsewhere in Matthew's gospel, however veiled those references are. Like an important clue, which makes itself known midway through a story, we only become aware of it as we approach the climax of the drama. Notice what Jesus said to His inner circle.

> And calling His twelve disciples, Jesus gave them authority over unclean spirits so they could drive them out and heal every disease...
>
> These twelve, Jesus sent out with the following instructions: "Don't go onto the road of the Gentiles or enter any town of the Samaritans. Go instead to the lost sheep of Israel. And as you go, preach this message: 'The Kingdom of Heaven is at hand.'"[122]

---

122 *Matthew 10:1-5-7*

And in case you think this reference to "lost sheep" was an aberration, Matthew made sure to further record:

> Leaving that place, Jesus withdrew to the district of Tyre and Sidon. And a Canaanite woman from that region came to Him, crying out, "Lord, Son of David, have mercy on me! My daughter is miserably possessed by a demon."
>
> But Jesus didn't answer her, so one of His disciples came and urged Him, "Send her away, because she keeps calling for us."
>
> He answered, "I was sent only to the lost sheep of the House of Israel."
>
> The woman came and knelt before Him. "Lord, help me!" she said.
>
> But Jesus replied, "It isn't right to take the children's bread and toss it to the dogs."
>
> "Yes, Lord," she said, "but even the dogs eat the crumbs that fall from their master's table."
>
> "Oh, woman," Jesus answered, "your faith is great! Let it be done for you as you desire." And her daughter was healed from that very hour.[123]

Two Families, Two Houses

SEVERAL IMPORTANT points make themselves known in the reading of these two pronouncements. To begin with, Jesus made it clear that these sheep to whom He referred were not, as many suggest, metaphorical "lost sheep." Rather, the sheep He and His disciples were sent to were, in fact, the lost sheep of the House of Israel.

Here we face the single greatest stumbling block in our quest to discover the *who* and the *where* of the people Moses, Nathan, and Daniel described. That's because many well-intentioned theologians and biblical historians misconstrue these passages by wrongly assuming that the House of Judah and the House of Israel are identical. But if they were identical, then why did the prophet Jeremiah say:

---

123   *Matthew 15:21-28*

"Look and see, the days are coming," declares the Lord, "when I'll fulfill the gracious promise that I've spoken to the House of Israel and to the House of Judah..."

Moreover, the word of the Lord came to Jeremiah: "Haven't you noticed what these people are saying: 'The Lord has rejected the two families He had chosen'?"[124]

And if they weren't two families, two houses, as opposed to just one, then why does *The Bible* tell us:

The Lord said, "I'll remove Judah also from My sight, just as I removed Israel. And I'll cast off Jerusalem, the city which I've chosen, and the Temple, of which I said, 'My name will be there.'"[125]

So when we fail to notice this distinction between the northern kingdom of Israel and the southern kingdom of Judah, we fail to understand that when Jesus said He'd been sent to the lost sheep of the House of Israel He'd first have to leave Palestine to go to them.

We also come face to face with another paradox when we have the courage to acknowledge it. Consider this: When Jesus told His disciples to avoid going onto the road of the Gentiles or enter any town of the Samaritans or when He initially refused to help the Canaanite woman, we should recognize that Jesus was contradicting His own example that He'd worked so hard to set for His disciples. Correct me if I'm wrong: When Jesus healed the Roman centurion's servant or told the parable of the Good Samaritan, wasn't He following in the footsteps of Abraham who didn't limit the call of God to a single race of people, as though the Hebrews were the only acceptable race in God's eyes? Isn't that why the Apostle Paul made it clear that the promise of grace preceded the giving of the Law by more than four centuries? True believers, in God's view, aren't those who are physically circumcised but those who are spiritually circumcised, as it were. True children of Abraham aren't those who are made perfect through their conforming to the Law of

---

124 Jeremiah 33:14, 23

125 Second Kings 23:27

Moses but through their believing in Christ Jesus, the same way that God imputed righteousness to Abraham. Certainly if Paul understood this, then Jesus understood it even more clearly.

What seems to be happening, then, when Jesus told His disciples to avoid the Gentiles, Samaritans, or Canaanites, is quite the opposite of what we think when we consider these prohibitions in a cursory manner. In other words, without really understanding what Jesus was saying about His being sent first to the lost sheep of the House of Israel, we misunderstand the intention of these prohibitions. But fortunately we no longer need to be controlled by this lack of understanding because we have Jesus' response to the Canaanite woman, who represented everyone Jesus told His disciples to avoid. And herein lies proof that we're dealing with a genuine paradox and not just another inconsistency that critics and skeptics love to point out to undermine our faith in God's word.

In healing the Canaanite woman's daughter, Jesus gave us the key to reinterpreting the meaning of the mission He bestowed upon His disciples. This is confirmed by the disciples' response to the persistence of the Canaanite woman who so irritated them that they begged Jesus to send her away. But as usual Jesus is far too sophisticated in His approach to life to do what His disciples expected Him to do.

In this, we'd do well to remember our original scene of the disciples asking Jesus to teach them to pray. As tradition would have us believe, when Jesus articulated His prayer, the disciples were entirely on board with it. But in light of the troubling times the disciples were facing at that time, we now understand they were really hoping for a much more radical approach to prayer. Far from hoping that God would provide mere bread and forgiveness, what they thought they needed was the power they saw Jesus wielding when He calmed the storm or walked on water. If that's true, then we can be just as certain that when the disciples asked Jesus to shoo away this irritating Canaanite woman, they were undoubtedly expecting Him to send her away empty-handed.

I mean, what else would He have done in light of His instructions to avoid the Gentiles or the Samaritans, or His initial response to the Canaanite woman? After all, hadn't He compared her to the dogs? Yet how few ever consider the implications of this scene? Instead of rebuking the Canaanite woman and sending her away, as the disciples had hoped for, Jesus responded in an unexpected way, just as He had when the people brought before Him the woman caught in adultery. Instead of refusing to help her, Jesus granted the request of this despised Canaanite woman and healed her daughter.

So why did He do that for her? Why didn't He send her away? Why did He seem to contradict His own edict to avoid such non-Jews? Of course, He did it because of her faith. Through faith, Jesus was able to impute to her the righteousness of God, regardless of her race, creed, or social position. Faith, in that respect, is the great equalizer in God's Universe, the thing that levels the playing field and unites all in all.

Scattered Among the Nations

IF THAT'S true, then how might we reinterpret Jesus' statement to the Canaanite woman that He couldn't help her because He'd only been sent to the lost sheep of Israel? In light of the fact that Jesus did help her because of her faith, I'd suggest His comments about His mission reveal far more than meets the eye. I'd suggest, in granting her request, Jesus not only upended the disciples' understanding of His mission to Judah, but He's also upended our understanding of His mission to these lost sheep.

That's because what people overlook is that it's impossible to understand this reference to lost sheep apart from the context of Jesus' statement that what was offered to the House of Judah was being taken from them and given to a nation that would bear fruit. As such, the purpose of Jesus' mission was to restart, in that "other place," the thing God had intended for Judah but which they forfeited when they rejected Him as the Messiah. Let me explain what I mean by that.

Keep in mind: If Jesus willingly embraced the Canaanite woman because of her exemplary faith, then Jesus' comments about avoiding the Gentiles or Samaritans didn't mean that, in going to these lost sheep, they should avoid them in the sense we might assume. If that were the case, then clearly the call of

Christ would be at cross-purposes with the grace of God as envisioned by Abraham, the great proselytizer and father of faith.

In this, we must remember why God called Abraham and his descendants in the first place. They were never supposed to be the only recipients of God's grace to the exclusion of all other peoples. Instead, God intended them to be channels to bless the whole world—Jews and non-Jews alike. And if that's true, then Jesus' mission wasn't one in which He and His disciples were going there to "convert" lost sheep, as if their so-called "lostness" spoke of their being lost in a spiritual sense. No, not by a long shot. Instead, when Jesus spoke of going to these lost ones, He was thinking in terms of their being lost because they had long ago been "divided" and "scattered," just as so many others before them had been punished and removed from their homeland.

Again and again, God's word declared that in Israel He'd be glorified among the nations of the world. But as *The Bible* records, when the united Kingdom of Israel, under King Solomon, was divided around 900 B.C., this split was a turning point in which one nation became two. The kingdom to the north, comprised of ten tribes, became known as the House of Israel, and the kingdom to the south, comprised of two tribes, became known as the House of Judah.

Eventually, the northern kingdom of Israel fell as a result of God's divine punishment because of their continued rebellion and idol worship, and in 722 B.C. the House of Israel was carried into captivity by the Assyrians. At this point in history, the northern kingdom of Israel became known ever after as the Lost Tribes of Israel, while the southern kingdom of Judah, although suffering a similar captivity at the hands of the Babylonians, remained intact.

It was this southern nation, then—the nation of the Jews— that existed until the time when Jesus was born and when the Scriptures speak of His "coming to His own but His own receiving Him not." It is in this context, and this context alone, that we can begin to penetrate the veil of Christ's hidden meaning when He revealed that He'd been sent first to the lost sheep of the House of Israel.

He wasn't sent to any old people who could be characterized as "lost sheep." These weren't merely wayward sinners in the traditional sense of how the term "lost sheep" is invoked by modern-day Christians to describe lost humanity in general. We're talking about what happened as a result of the House of Judah rejecting Jesus' call to accept Him as their Messiah. Instead of activating the next phase of God's purpose for them to be the channel of blessing to the whole world, Jesus reassigned the mission back upon the northern kingdom of the House of Israel, which had many centuries earlier been carried into captivity and subsequently scattered among the nations of the world, never to be heard from again—or so it would've seemed.

While most consider the story of the Lost Tribes of Israel to be meritless in the overall scheme of biblical history, we now know this to be false. To the contrary, in light of God's stated purpose, in which He separated the sons of Adam, and set the boundaries of the nations according to the number of the Children of Jacob, the scattering of Israel constitutes the linchpin of human history. And so, in dividing these dust-like descendants, God ordained that His people be dispersed throughout the world, so that in their outcast state they will then, and only then, accomplish God's call to be a blessing to the whole Earth.

If these critical aspects are incorporated into our search, then by all means, we can proceed in asking: Where are these so-called "lost sheep of the House of Israel" of which Jesus spoke? Are they so lost that not even God can find them? How can we be sure these lost ones are the same people of the northern kingdom of Israel who disappeared from world history in 722 B.C.? How do we demonstrate from the historical record that these are the same people of which Moses, Nathan, Daniel, and Jesus spoke? And finally, in locating these "lost sheep," have we come at last upon the historical link we've been looking for in trying to connect Israel of old and America today?

CHAPTER FOURTEEN

AS CORN IS SIFTED IN A SIEVE

*See how I observe this sinful kingdom, having
destroyed it from the face of the Earth, though
I haven't utterly wiped out the House of Jacob.
Look at how I've commanded, so that I'll sift
the House of Israel throughout every nation,
as corn is sifted in a sieve, yet I haven't lost
track of a single grain. (Amos 9:8-9)*

The Stage Was Set for a New Chapter

BUT KING Solomon loved many strange women;[126] so says *The Bible*, speaking of the same man who had once been called the wisest man in the world. The wisdom of Solomon was said to have been as measureless as the sand on the seashore, greater than all the wisdom of the East, greater than all of Egypt. He was said to have written three hundred proverbs and more than a thousand songs. Solomon was so wise, in fact, that people from every nation in the ancient world came to hear him speak, among them, the fabled Queen of Sheba.[127] Solomon, son of David, and builder of the splendors of the Temple of God at Jerusalem; Solomon, the man who loved many strange women, and whose many wives eventually turned

---

126   *First Kings 11:1*

127   *Ibid. 4:29-34; 10:1-13*

his heart after other gods.[128]

So the Lord became angry with Solomon, because in his old age his heart turned away from the God of Israel, so He told him:

> Because you've done this thing … I will tear the kingdom away from you and give it to one of your own officials. But for the sake of your father David, I won't do this while you're alive, but I'll tear it out of the hand of your son. Still, I won't tear the whole kingdom from him, but I'll give him one tribe for My servant David's sake and for the sake of Jerusalem, which I've chosen.[129]

In this way, Solomon went from being the wisest man in the world, unmatched in wealth, power, and prestige, to the man who was responsible for dividing the Kingdom of Israel that had stood united for more than a hundred years. Thus, the stage was set for a new chapter in the drama of God's people.

In This Most Peculiar Way

AND WHAT a drama it's been, from the moment that Moses led the Israelites through the parted Red Sea, through forty years of wandering through the Wilderness en route to their new home, with just a slight detour at Mount Sinai along the way. Then, triumphantly entering the Promised Land after having conquered the land under the leadership of Joshua, the Israelites settled there—a chosen people separated to their God.

At first, they were ruled by a series of judges, by the likes of Gideon, Jephthah, Deborah, and Samson. But afterward, the people demanded a king to rule over them; and although God preferred being their King, He eventually relented and provided them with a dynasty of human kings—first Saul, then David, then his son Solomon.

And although the people of Israel seemed at first to have gotten what they'd wished for, there was never a time in the history of these kings that there wasn't some form of controversy.

---

128   *First Kings 11:4*

129   *Ibid. 11:9, 11-13*

The issue came down to just one thing: Could a nation borne by the miraculous intervention of a Supreme Being be ruled by that same Deity—whether by His own hand or through some human intermediary?

To this day, the answer remains very much in question.

Then, sometime in the days after Solomon had received word that God would be dividing the kingdom, one of his officials by the name of Jeroboam had been traveling just outside of Jerusalem. As it turns out, this man had so impressed Solomon in a recent building project in Jerusalem that the old king had put Jeroboam in charge of the entire working force of the tribes of Joseph.

This day, Jeroboam was strolling along, dressed in a new coat, feeling very satisfied about his new station in life, both courtesy of King Solomon, when suddenly a strange-looking fellow stepped up to him.

"Hello, Jeroboam," the strange man said. "I'm so glad, so glad I finally found you."

"Me? Why me?" replied Jeroboam, squinting in the harsh glare of the midday Sun, trying to size up this odd fellow. "Who are you?"

"I am Ahijah … from Shiloh… I'm called Ahijah, yes?"

Mulling this over for several moments, Jeroboam's eyes then lit up. "Ahijah … ah, yes, of Shiloh, you say… Are you *the* Ahijah, then? Ahijah, the prophet?"

"I am, sir," Ahijah said, respectfully nodding his head.

Jeroboam nodded back. "So nice to meet you, my friend."

"You've heard about me, then? Is that what you're saying?"

"Certainly; who in Jerusalem hasn't?" Jeroboam replied, then suddenly grew uneasy. "Say, what's this all about, anyway?"

"I have a message for you—that's what this is about."

"A message … for me? From who?"

"The Holy One of Israel, that's who—the Lord God Himself!"

Stunned, Jeroboam's eyes thinned. "The Lord God? What on Earth are you talking about? What message?"

Without warning, Ahijah thrust his hands forward and

grabbed hold of Jeroboam's new coat.

"For God's sake, man!" Jeroboam snorted. "What are you doing? Keep your hands off me!"

A struggled then ensued as each man jockeyed for position, but clearly this odd-looking fellow was much stronger than Jeroboam had anticipated and before he knew it, the man—this prophet of God?—had removed his coat. And before Jeroboam could say another word, Ahijah started tearing the coat to pieces right before his gaping eyes.

"You crazy fool!" barked Jeroboam. "That was a brand-new coat! King Solomon just gave it to me! Have you lost your mind?"

Tearing the coat into a dozen pieces, Ahijah handed Jeroboam most of them. "Here; you take ten pieces for yourself. This is what the Lord says: I'm going to tear the kingdom out of Solomon's hand and give you ten tribes." Ahijah then held up the last two pieces in his hand for Jeroboam to see. "But for the sake of My servant David and My city Jerusalem, his son will get one tribe. As for you, Jeroboam, I'm making you king over Israel; and if you obey Me as David did, I'll be with you. And in the days to come, you watch: I'll build you a dynasty as enduring as the one I built for David."[130]

In this most peculiar way, God, through the prophet Ahijah, sparked off the revolution that would divide the kingdom, around 900 B.C., with the ten tribes of Israel to the north and the two tribes of Judah to the south. For the next two hundred years, the northern kingdom of Israel would see the rise and fall of nineteen kings, springing from nine different dynastic families. The southern kingdom of Judah would follow a much different pattern, though just as troublesome. For more than three hundred years, they would see the ascension of nineteen kings and one queen, all originating from the line of David.

Eventually, as a form of divine punishment, both kingdoms were destroyed by invading armies, with the House of Israel being carried away by the Assyrians around 722 B.C. and the House of Judah, by the Babylonians around 586 B.C. But whereas the House of Judah remained fairly intact during their

---

130   *First Kings 11:29-38*

Babylonian captivity, it was the unique fate of the House of Israel to receive the specific judgment of being scattered throughout the nations. That's when, according to the traditional view of history, the northern ten tribes seemed to vanish from the face of the Earth, and why they became known ever after as the Lost Tribes of Israel.

No Longer My People

BUT IS THAT really the final chapter to the story? Is tradition correct in its view that these so-called "lost tribes" are gone forever, never to be seen or heard from again? Or does *The Bible* actually portray a far different picture?

As I see it, there are three questions we need to answer if we're to solve this age-old mystery. One, why did God scatter the House of Israel amongst the nations in the first place? Two, if these northern tribes were lost to history, does that mean God lost track of them, too? And three, is it God's intention that they remain lost forever?

First, let's look at what else the Scriptures have to say about why God scattered the northern House of Israel. In *The Book of Leviticus*, we find the origin of God's intention toward them, when He said:

> I am the Lord your God Who rescued you from Egypt so that you'd no longer be slaves to them... But if you resist My laws, hate My statutes, and scorn My judgments… I'll oppose you, and you'll be destroyed by your enemies. And if you refuse to obey Me, I'll punish you seven times more for your sins.[131]

This same idea repeats three more times, in the next ten verses, and then God said:

> And if, in spite of all these things, you still refuse to listen to Me … then I'll *scatter* you among the heathen, and your cities will lie desolate.[132]

131　Leviticus 26:13, 15, 17-18

132　Ibid. 26:33

But why would God do something like that? Why doesn't He just punish the people and be done with it? Why does He have to remove them from the land, too? The next passage explains why.

> Then the land will finally enjoy the Sabbaths as long as your land lies desolate and you remain in the land of your enemies. As long as your land remains uninhabitable, then it will rest, even as it didn't rest during the time that you lived there.[133]

So, there's the answer to our first question. God scattered the people of Israel so the land would be able to fulfill His plan—in this case, concerning the much-misunderstood concept of the Sabbath rest, which typifies what *The Book of Hebrews* speaks of when it describes the rest that follows the work of faith.

> We who have had faith have entered into that rest. Whereas God spoke in another place about the seventh day in this regard: "And God rested on the seventh day from all His works." Therefore, there remains a rest for the people of God, because whoever enters into His rest has also ceased from his own works, just as God did from His.[134]

In other words, when God's people live according to the precepts of faith, they, too, can expect to rest in that accomplishment, even as God rested on the seventh day of His creation. This, then, is the true meaning of Sabbath rest.

The real significance of this is, for most of the time the Children of Israel lived in Palestine, they'd lost sight of why God had placed them there. They weren't there for their sakes alone; God had a greater purpose in mind, a purpose they eventually squandered. That's why God removed them from the land, so they might finally turn from their old ways of disobedience, which could only happen after they were carried away into captivity. Only then could the Israelites return to the kind of faith they'd forgotten about after so many years of false religion, fostered by

---

133   Leviticus 26:34-35

134   Hebrews 4:3-4, 10

the belief that they'd always be God's darlings, no matter what they did to provoke Him.

That said, one more thing needs to be mentioned here, in the context of God's dividing, scattering, and uniting of His people. Typically, when God's word speaks of the scattering of His chosen ones, the words we've seen so far all hearken back to the days of Noah being told to spread out across the face of the Earth. In the case of Nimrod, this spreading out was an important factor in counteracting humanity's habit of consolidating power as a prelude to abusing that power. But in these verses in *Leviticus*, God introduced another dimension to this scattering effort. And again, this added dimension is one that's completely lost when looking at these verses in English. That's because when we look at the Hebrew word used here for this "scattering," a startling insight leaps out at us, in the context of all we've learned about God's ultimate purpose in dispersing the sheep of His pasture.

On the surface, we only see a God Who seems more interested in punishing sinners than rehabilitating them. This, of course, has always been a bone of contention with critics and skeptics alike, when God repeatedly, in *The Old Testament*, spoke more about judgment than He did about mercy. But not so when we re-examine these verses in *Leviticus* in the context of what we've established to this point.

When Moses said that if the Israelites refused to obey God He'd scatter them among the heathen, and their cities would lie desolate, the Hebrew word he used for "scatter" wasn't *parad*, *parar*, *palag*, or *puwts*, as in previous cases. The word he used was *ezareh*, from the root word *zara*, which as we learned in an earlier chapter spoke not only of being "scattered" but also of being "sown as light."

So here again we see God's word revealing that while the devil and his minions no doubt considered Israel's failure a victory on their part, this failure actually became a doorway of hope for the rest of humanity. As in, when God warned His people of the consequences of their unwillingness to obey His laws, one of two things would happen: One, they'd obey and live happily in the land that God had given them, and in their being a "beacon of light" to the nations, they'd become a blessing to humanity in that act of obedience; or, two, they'd disobey and be driven from the land that God had given them, and in their being "scattered as light" amongst the nations, they'd become a blessing to humanity in that act of disobedience.

The next question is: Once the northern tribes of Israel were carried away into captivity, did God lose track of them in their lost condition? The prophet Amos gives us a hint of God's perspective of this global drama.

> See how I observe this sinful kingdom, having destroyed it from the face of the Earth, though I haven't utterly wiped out the House of Jacob. Look at how I've commanded, so that I'll sift the House of Israel throughout every nation, as corn is sifted in a sieve, yet I haven't lost track of a single grain.[135]

From this passage we see that while humans may have lost track of the Lost Tribes of Israel, God never lost track of them. The prophet Hosea confirmed this, when he had God saying, "Israel isn't hidden from Me, for I see that she's defiled."[136]

This becomes even more obvious when we take the time to put the words of Amos into the overall context of our present investigation. When Amos spoke of God's intent to sift the House of Israel as corn is sifted, he used two Hebrew words that are variations of the root word *nua*—as in, to "sift," where the word is *wahaniowti*, and then, as corn is "sifted" in a sieve, where the word is *yinnowa*. In this word *nua*, we see several familiar associated meanings, such as to "scatter," "shake," and "wander." Moses also used a variant of this word when he described God making the Children of Israel to "wander" for forty years in the Wilderness.[137]

Especially noteworthy is that the Hebrew word *yinnowa* bears a strong resemblance to an English word we've seen associated with why God scattered Israel; that word is to "winnow." God didn't scatter the House of Israel to erase them from histo-

---

135   Amos 9:8-9

136   Hosea 5:3

137   Numbers 32:13

ry, as is commonly assumed. We know this because of that other Hebrew word that keeps coming to the fore—*zara*—which also has as one of its meanings, to "winnow." Far from intending to annihilate Israel in this scattering, shaking, and wandering process, God was winnowing them, as one separates chaff from grain, or insects from stored grain. Through the mouth of Hosea, God said to the rebellious tribes of the north:

> Therefore, they will be like the morning mist, like the early dew that vanishes, like chaff blown from a threshing floor, like smoke through an open window.[138]

Taken together, we see in these verses that even while the Israelites as a whole refused to live up to their potential, God knew exactly how to sort out the kernels worth saving from amongst those that were not. In this shaking process, in causing them to wander, this sifting process winnowed out the faithless from the faithful. And in this way, God scattered the useful grain of Israel throughout the nations, as light is scattered to enlighten the whole world in due time. In short, what God did on a regional level, with Israel's forty-year wandering in the Sinai Desert, He then did on a global level, with the northern House of Israel, subsequent to the Assyrian Captivity in 722 B.C.

In fact, God was so intent on this global drama of Israel's scattering that He called the prophet Hosea to do the unthinkable. Just as Ahijah had done before him, in driving his point home to Jeroboam by tearing his coat into twelve pieces, God would, with Hosea, up the ante even further. Sometime after the reign of Jeroboam ended around 746 B.C., in the years leading up to the downfall of the northern kingdom, the Lord rammed His message down the proverbial throat of an entire nation by having Hosea marry a prostitute! Then He had Hosea name his three children by this woman according to a specific aspect of divine judgment that would soon overtake them because of their idolatry and disobedience.

And Hosea's wife bore him a son whom he named Jezreel, because God said, "Soon I'll cause the Kingdom of

---

138   Hosea 13:3

Israel to cease."

Then his wife bore him a daughter whom he named Loruhamah, because God said, "I'll no longer have mercy on the House of Israel, but will allow them to be carried away into captivity."

And finally, his wife gave birth to another son whom he named Loammi, because God said, "You're no longer My people, and I won't be your God."[139]

So, if you think Jeroboam was shocked when Ahijah handed him ten pieces of what had just been his new coat, just imagine the stunned look on the faces of those Israelites when they saw one of God's own prophets had married a whore—and had three kids by her, to boot! The only thing more shocking, I'm sure, would've been the look on any of the faces of those who'd come to understand what God was saying to them through Hosea's actions.

Fortunately for all involved, though, the story of Israel's disgrace was destined to not end on such a dismal note, because, as bizarre as it appeared to the uninitiated, the Lord was still working out an important purpose in all of this.

Once again, a closer look at the word meanings of those involved in this drama of Hosea and his children reveals so much more than meets the eye. When God told Hosea to name his first son Jezreel, we should, by now, be most intrigued to discover that the name Jezreel comes from a combination of two other root words. According to *Strong's Exhaustive Concordance*, Jezreel comes from *zara* for "sows" and from *el* for "God." Therefore, Jezreel means "God sows."

So, when we only look to the English translation of *The Bible*, we might assume God sowed Israel to hide them in the ground where they'd be lost to history, or scattered them to have them absorbed by every other nation, as tradition so persistently insists. But not so when we understand the underlying meaning of the *zara* component to the name Jezreel. In God's naming of Hosea's first son Jezreel, a divine message was being relayed to those with eyes to see: Although God's judgment of the House

---

139 *Hosea 1:4-9*

of Israel was painfully bitter to them, God's act of dividing and scattering His people was actually one in which the rest of the world was inseminated with the true light that only the Lord could see within the potential of His "lost"—but not forgotten—"sheep."

We know this because, even in the midst of Hosea's pronouncements of punishment and rejection, as characterized in the names of his other two children, Loruhamah and Loammi, another word of God came to Him. Just when all hope seemed lost, God interjected a remarkable twist to this ongoing drama—a grand soap opera of the ages, if you will. Without even pausing between sentences, Hosea then prophesied of that day when Israel's downfall would finally lead to a new day of hope and restoration. On the heels of the previous passages of doom, the prophet declared:

> Yet the number of the Children of Israel will be as the sand of the sea that cannot be measured or numbered, and someday, in the very place where it was said, "You're not My people," even there it will be said, "You are the children of the Living God."[140]

This provides the answer, then, to our third question: No, God doesn't intend for the northern kingdom of Israel to remain lost forever. Though once a disgrace among the nations of the world, Israel, the desolate, Israel, the scattered, will one day be the recipient of one of God's greatest acts of mercy and redemption. More importantly, not only were they to become so much more than they were before they were scattered, but this divine gift would also take the Abrahamic promise of dust-like descendants to a whole new level, and with it, the promise that the whole Earth would be blessed as well.

These Long-Lost People

"BUT WHEN," you might ask, "will these 'lost sheep' be rediscovered? Has it already happened? Will it occur in our lifetime? Or is it likely to occur at some future point in time?"

---

140 *Hosea 1:10*

Believe it or not, the answer involves not so much the theology of *The Bible* but, rather, the science of archeology. It was during the mid-1800s that this amazing science of uncovering the past began to discover where in the world the Lost Tribes of Israel had disappeared after they'd been taken into captivity. As if from out of nowhere, the discoveries made famous by men like Henry Rawlinson and Austen Henry Layard began to blow the lid off the whereabouts of these long-lost people. Almost overnight, what had been considered merely myth began to, slowly but surely, edge its way into the arena of factual history.

Between 1835 and 1839, Rawlinson copied and translated an inscription on an ancient rock relief located in western Iran, which bore an account authored by Darius the Great, the Persian king best known for his role in the rebuilding of Jerusalem after the Babylonian Captivity. It's this relief, known as the Behistun Inscription, which provided the linguistic keys to determine the historical roots of the Lost Tribes of Israel. On it, three parallel narratives, written in Persian, Babylonian, and Scythian, describe events in the history of these scattered tribes, giving historians their first glimpse into the much sought after jumping-off point of these mysterious people.

Next came Layard, who, in 1847, unearthed the Assyrian capital of Nineveh and with it, the royal library of the Assyrian kings, which contained a vast array of clay tablets. Written in the seventh century B.C., these tablets contained cuneiform texts referring to the captive Israelites. Tying together all the data gathered via these unparalleled feats of archeology, scholars soon learned that the people whom *The Bible* says were captured and relocated to Assyria had actually remained a distinct and vibrant people. In time, this new group, known as the *Skythai*, or Scythians, multiplied so quickly and exerted such an influence that, within a hundred years or so, they broke free from captivity to become the people that history now records as the *Keltoi*, or Celts, of Europe.

According to historians, the first reference to these *Keltoi* was by the Greek geographer Hecataeus in 571 B.C., who, in giving them this name, has provided us with a telling clue as to their true origins. To some it might seem incidental, but certainly not to those who believe that, when the God of *The Bible* says something, He means it. As it so happens, *Keltoi*, say these same historians, comes from the Indo-European root word *kel*, which means "hidden."

Of course, there are always those who would insist that none of this is even possible because once God punished them they were supposed to remain hidden, to wander life ever after as outcasts among the nations into which they were scattered. But not according to the prophet Jeremiah, who saw a far different fate for them:

> For Israel is not forsaken, or Judah, of their God; though their land is full of guilt against the Holy One of Israel... You are My battle-axe and weapons of war, and with you, I'll break in pieces the nations. With you, I'll destroy kingdoms, and with you, I'll break in pieces the horse and the rider.[141]

Far from being timid nomads, the Celts were fierce warriors that swept across the European continent, in wave after irresistible wave, terrorizing even the legions of Rome. They eventually grew so plentiful that they split into innumerable factions—among them: Gauls, Goths, Picts, Angles, Saxons, and Jutes. As such, these prodigious nations—as populous "as the sand of the sea"—came to inhabit the whole of Europe, including England, Scotland, Wales, Ireland, Brittany, Holland, Belgium, France, Spain, Portugal, Denmark, Sweden, Norway, Finland, Italy, and Germany.

So much can be said about these vast migrations and the many volumes of scholarship concerning them that this work could never encompass it all. Suffice it to say, the cultural connections have been made, and they've been done by some of the most prolific scholars in the annals of history. For the sake of this work, however, what we've provided still makes the point abundantly clear: Yes, God in His righteous indignation punished the northern House of Israel with dispersion. Yes, He even blinded them with a temporary form of "national amnesia," as it were. But never did He intend to leave them in a permanent

---

state of derision and destitution. As depicted in His word of promise and as revealed through the timely establishment of the science of archeology, both bear witness to God's unique ability to guide and nurture those people who are called by His name.

Thus, it appears the prophecy of Hosea has actually come true, and with it, another of the greatest misconceptions ever blamed on *The Bible* has come crashing down. After all, we only need to ask a series of questions to verify the preceding statements: Where did the message of Christianity spread like wildfire if not in every one of the nations just mentioned? And if not in those nations—though once hidden, yet restored in the fullness of time—then where else would you suggest that it was more fervently received? And if they did embrace the Gospel of Christ brought to them by ambassadors of truth like the Apostle Paul and his group, then what greater proof is there to verify the fulfillment of Hosea's prophecy?

As it was written, and as it undoubtedly came to pass:

Yet the number of the Children of Israel will be as the sand of the sea, which cannot be measured or numbered. And someday, in the very place where it was said, "You're not My people," it will be said, "You are the children of the Living God."[142]

---

142   *Hosea 1:10*

C H A P T E R   F I F T E E N

UNDER THE DEVIL'S RADAR

> *For our struggle isn't against flesh and
> blood but against the rulers, against the
> authorities, against the powers of this
> world's darkness, and against the spiritual
> forces of evil in the heavenly realms.*
> *(Ephesians 6:12)*

Who to Attack Next

IN THIS timeless pattern of the dividing, scattering, and uniting of God's people, we actually see much more than we'd expect to see. Naturally, when looking to all things biblical, we see God using this pattern to purge and perfect the sheep of His pasture. However, God's actions aren't the only things we see; just as importantly, we also see Satan's actions in all of it. In short, when the devil sees God commission someone to spread His truth to the whole world, he knows what even the human participants of this divine drama never suspect at the time; Satan knows exactly who to attack next in this ages-long tug of war between him and God.

The idea of the devil being made aware of whom God calls goes a long way in explaining why God sometimes performs His miracles in a grand, public manner, and why He sometimes performs them in a modest, private manner. This explains why God sometimes reveals who on the world stage are His chosen

168

ones, and why He sometimes hides an awareness of that calling. That's why, in every case, God employs His set times to run a very specific period, at the conclusion of which humanity comes alive to something previously hidden in the counsels of Heaven. It also explains why even though God was grieved when the Jews of Jesus' day rejected Him, He knew how to rework events so they'd still play into His larger plan for humanity as a whole.

It was the same plan God introduced to Abraham and Sarah, who were the recipients of the "birthright promises," the true scope of which they could never begin to imagine. It was the same plan bequeathed to Abraham's children, which was that the birthright promises weren't given to them for their own personal gain; they were given so they could be channeled to bless the whole world.

So when Abraham received those blessings, he began the journey knowing full well that it was his job to share those blessings. This is certainly borne out by the biblical record that has Abraham eager to proselytize others into the faith of the God of his forefathers. Unlike later generations, who became more and more insular, more and more exclusive, Abraham began his calling doing things God's way, in spreading the truth of the Divine to everyone he met. But as the power of the birthright blessing grew in sweep and magnitude, it became increasingly clear that its power to curse was often greater than its power to bless.

Just look at what happened in the case of Abraham's grandson Jacob and his immediate family. Instead of living in peace and harmony, as would be expected of the sons of Jacob, they grew as jealous of each other as any of the sons of disobedience. It wasn't as though God slighted any of Jacob's sons; all twelve of them received their own unique blessings from On High. Most notably, Judah was blessed with the scepter, with which his children would rule and reign on behalf of the family. Levi was blessed with the priesthood, with which his children would minister the things of God on behalf of the family. And Dan was given power over the seas and blessed with a talent for establishing his name wherever his children went in their maritime travels. Yet none of those personal blessings seemed to be enough for any of the brothers, especially after their younger brother Joseph, quite innocently and naively, began to tell them about a series of dreams he'd been having.

> "Look," said Joseph, "I had another dream last night. This time the Sun, the Moon and eleven stars bowed down to me."
>
> And when Joseph told this to his brothers, his father Jacob overheard him and rebuked him, saying, "What's this dream you've had? Do you actually think your mother and brothers and I will ever come and bow down before you?"
>
> And his brothers became more and more jealous of him.[143]

Eventually Joseph's brothers became so angry with him, they intended to kill him. But fortunately, the oldest brother Reuben talked them out of it at the last minute, and instead they threw Joseph into a pit until they could decide next what to do with him. Only later did Judah convince his brothers that killing Joseph was out of the question, and that's when they sold him to Egyptian slave-traders.

So what happened as a result of this jealousy and hatred, when the thing that was supposed to bless Jacob's sons nearly cursed them instead? What did God do, when Joseph's brothers short-circuited His plan that they carry on their grandfather's work of blessing the whole world? Of course, God used it to His advantage by redirecting events so Joseph—in the role of outsider turned deliverer—would learn a great lesson of humility before elevating him as the viceroy of Egypt. And God did the same thing with his jealous brothers by striking the land of Canaan with famine, which then drove Jacob's entire family down to Egypt, where they were forced to humbly submit to the viceroy to save their starving children.

In setting the stage this way, for the exodus of Israel under Moses—also in the role of outsider as deliverer—the words of Hosea would be fulfilled: "When Israel was a child, I loved him, and out of Egypt I called my son."[144]

---

143   Genesis 37:9-10

144   Hosea 11:1

To Play Out Privately

WE SEE THE same thing, in how the House of Israel's disobedience in the Promised Land became a jumping-off point for the next chapter of biblical history. In 722 B.C. when Assyria removed the northern kingdom of Israel from their portion of Palestine, their downfall became God's opportunity to scatter them in an unexpected way. Although the devil undoubtedly thought he'd won the day by bringing down the kingdom to the north, God had other intentions for these "lost sheep."

The same thing happened again in 586 B.C. when Babylon sacked Jerusalem and the people of the southern kingdom of Judah were taken into captivity for seventy years. Once again, while the devil thought he'd prevailed in foiling God's plan of the ages, he merely triggered yet another forced migration of outsiders, outliers, and aliens, also with unexpected results—two of them, actually.

The first migration involved a public event, that of the return of the Jews from Babylon after seventy years of captivity. This event is well documented in *The Old Testament*, while a second migration during the same period of history isn't so well known. That's because while the Jewish migration back to Palestine, led by Ezra and Nehemiah, was played out publicly, to confirm God's faithfulness in regard to what the Seventy Weeks of Daniel communicates, the second migration was ordained to play out privately. And while we read of this private migration in *The Book of Jeremiah*, as having occurred after the fall of Jerusalem but prior to the Babylonian Captivity, the story of this migration is so threadbare that most biblical scholars overlook it to this day. And it's been overlooked for several reasons.

First, because this migration is conveyed in such veiled terms, it doesn't draw attention to itself. Unlike the sweeping drama of the sacking of Jerusalem and the deportation of thousands of Judahites into captivity, this other migration contained very little in the way of high drama. However, in terms of our present investigation, it turns out to have far more real drama built into it than most care to admit. That's because, just as He did with the scattering of the so-called "lost sheep of the House of Israel," God chose this particular migration to be another of those that would fly "under the devil's radar," so to speak. Why?

It all goes back to the fact that whenever God publicly reveals the choice of His calling, that calling isn't made clear to just the human participants involved in that calling. It's also made clear to Satan, the archenemy of God, who then knows exactly who to attack next. In the case of the sons of the birthright promises, as soon as God declared, "Jacob I loved, but Esau I hated,"[145] the devil knew upon whom to focus his all-out warfare. When God chose Judah to be the vessel of the kingship of Israel, Satan specifically targeted him. When God ordained Levi to bear the priestly line, the devil set out to spoil that, too. And when God gave Joseph the rest of what the birthright promises held out for Abraham and his descendants, Satan wasted no time setting out to destroy Joseph's life. What better explanation do you have for the intense hatred and jealousy of Joseph's brothers? You don't think God chose the twelve sons of Jacob because they were petty, foolish men, do you? Certainly you see we're dealing with the same thing of which all students of *The Bible* are aware.

It's just as the Apostle Paul warned us concerning the invisible yet tangible forces of evil in this world—wicked, inhuman forces that seek to destroy and kill anyone who dares to seek the Lord in spirit and in truth.

> For our struggle isn't against flesh and blood but against the rulers, against the authorities, against the powers of this world's darkness, and against the spiritual forces of evil in the heavenly realms.[146]

That's why although God often reveals His choice of an individual publicly, this isn't always the case. Sometimes, for His plan to move forward, God needs to hide His plan from the devil; He needs to run it underground, to go undercover. Perhaps something of this way of thinking inspired the old Irish blessing: "May your glass be ever full. May the roof over your head be always strong. And may you be in Heaven half an hour before the devil knows you're dead."

---

145 Romans 9:13

146 Ephesians 6:12

Now while many might object to my suggestion that God has to trick the devil to defeat him, I assure you I'm not saying God hides the details of His plan because He lacks the power to destroy the devil with a blast of His nostrils. What I am suggesting, though, is that God knows all too well the nature of the devil's warfare against humanity. Satan knows he can't fool anyone who is trying to follow God's call by showing his true face; he only succeeds by way of deception and lies, by stealth and counterfeit. Therefore, in like manner, God has decided to cancel out the stealth and lies of the devil with His own version of subterfuge. Thus, for every lie of Satan, God counters with the ambiguity of His word, and for every counterfeit of the devil, the Lord counters with the paradox of His promises. That's why the Scriptures—which constitute a genuine coded message in the context of spiritual warfare—are so thoroughly couched in ambiguity and paradox. That's why, in this context of spiritual warfare, we should both recognize and appreciate the parallel between the hidden meanings in Scripture and the private aspects of biblical history.

I mean, it's not as though God can't communicate His truth in Scripture in a simple, straightforward manner, yet He doesn't. The same could be said of biblical history. It, too, could be spelled out in clear, unambiguous terms, yet it's not. Actually, it's for our sake that God both reveals and hides His truth in Scripture and in history, to outsmart the devil and win the war of the ages. Instead of having His prophetic word explain everything, clearly and obviously, He forces us to discern its meaning from its dark and often poetic language. That's why it's so easy for us to forget that everything we really know about the meaning of *The Bible* has come to us strictly after the fact. Which is just another way of saying that we really only understand what biblical prophecy tells us after it's been fulfilled and never before, although this fundamental fact of understanding Scripture is downplayed to such a huge degree.

The Curse of Knowledge

IN THIS, most theologians and historians suffer from what epistemologists call the Curse of Knowledge, whereby individuals "in the know" are so steeped in what they know about a given subject, they can no longer recapture a sense of what it's like to *not know* what they *know*.

Oddly enough, then, because experts know so much about biblical history, most overlook the possibility that what they know can actually prevent them from learning anything new about *The Bible*. And because of the ambiguous nature of Scripture, many biblical passages remain ambiguous until the truth seeker gains new information that enables him or her to see the same old passage in a brand-new way. It's not as though the passage itself changes; what changes is the mindset of the seeker who incorporates something new into his or her perspective, which then allows them to reinterpret the meaning of an old passage thereby turning it into a "new" one.

Those of you who think what I'm describing is absurd, ask yourself: Where in *The Old Testament* can you find any prophecies about the First Coming or the Second Coming of the Lord? The answer is: You can't find any, because the prophets only spoke from their perspective, which means that because of the ambiguity of God's word, the multifaceted nature of the Coming of the Lord was unknown to them. They never spoke of the "First Coming" or the "Second Coming." They only spoke of the "Day of the Lord" or the "Coming of the Son of Man." This explains why the people in Jesus' day were so baffled by His references to future aspects of this "Coming," because in their minds it comprised just one event, in which the Kingdom of God was to be established once and for all time, instead of how Christians now speak of it in light of history having filled in the details we've taken for granted ever since.

The same thing applies to the marriage between a man and a woman as speaking of the union between Christ and the Church, which was never specifically mentioned in *The Old Testament*. Marriage was mentioned, of course, but never had it been viewed in terms of a relationship between God and humanity. Then, as if from out of thin air, Paul tuned into a hidden frequency that had been built into God's word all along, when he quoted a familiar passage and saw a new meaning in it never before detected.

> For this reason a man will leave his father and mother and be united to his wife, and the two will become one flesh. This mystery is profound, but I'm speaking about Christ and the Church.[147]

But because marriage had never been described in these terms prior to Paul making this connection, he naturally called it a mystery. As *Barnes' Notes on The Bible* explains:

> The word "mystery"—*musterion*—means something which is concealed, hidden, before unknown; something into which one must be "initiated" or instructed before he can understand it. It does not mean that it is "incomprehensible" when it is disclosed, but that hitherto it has been kept secret. When disclosed it may be as intelligible as any other truth.

Even more mysterious than the idea that marriage represents the union between Christ and the Church is the idea of the Church itself. Just as the true nature of the Day of the Lord was beyond the prophets' ability to understand, the mystery of the Church was also something they never fully comprehended. It's not as though they weren't hinting at it when they prophesied that one day God's promises would extend to so many more than just the sons of Jacob. After all, prophecies like this are exactly what we've been tracing throughout this work:

> No longer will you be called Abram; your name will be Abraham, because I've made you a father of many nations.[148]

> You are My servant, Israel, in whom I will display My glory... I will also make you a light for the nations, to bring My salvation to the ends of the Earth.[149]

> So I tell you, the Kingdom of God will be taken from you and given to a nation that will bear fruit.[150]

---

147   Ephesians 5:31-32

148   Genesis 17:5

149   Isaiah 49:3, 6

150   Matthew 21:43

The Scriptures foresaw that God would justify the Gentiles by faith, and foretold the gospel to Abraham: "All nations will be blessed through you."[151]

Here we have four pivotal witnesses—Moses, Isaiah, Matthew, and Paul—all providing clues to "a mystery that was hidden for ages and generations but is now revealed to His saints."[152] The mystery of Christ's Church was that a body of non-Jewish believers was to be grafted into the tree of salvation that was originally thought to be intended only for the Children of Israel. Prior to the gospel age, it was considered unthinkable that the Gentiles could receive anything from the God of Abraham.

Ironically, though, the so-called "mystery" of this ingrafting of foreigners into the tree of Israel turns out to only be a mystery to those who never paid attention to all the clues that have been hidden in plain sight since time immemorial. What do I mean by that?

Well, look at the four passages just cited, in which Abraham is called the father of many "nations," Israel is to be a light for the "nations," Jesus gives the Kingdom of God to a "nation" that will bear fruit, and all "nations" are to be blessed through the gospel. According to *Strong's Exhaustive Concordance*, the Hebrew word translated as "nation" is *goy*, while in the Greek, "nation" is *ethnos*, both of which speak of Gentile or heathen nations.

Just think of it: All these years we've heard that Israel would be a light and a blessing to the Gentiles and heathen, and we say, sure, I can see that. But when was the last time you considered *The Bible* is also hinting that Abraham was a father of said Gentiles and heathen, or that Jesus would hand over the Kingdom of God to them?

Clearly, then, subjects like the Day of the Lord, marriage, and the Church all confirm the idea that not every truth of Scripture is immediately obvious. To the contrary, many require both time and scrutiny to expose their latent meaning. So when critics and skeptics ridicule anyone looking to solve the mystery

---

151 *Galatians 3:8*

152 *Colossians 1:26*

of these "other people" or that "other place," which the prophets clearly talked about, they should never abandon such a quest on the grounds that if God's word had anything to say on the subject, it would be made more obvious.

After all, is anyone suggesting that God rolled out the knowledge of the Trinity in chapter one of Scripture? Certainly not; instead, the knowledge of God the Father, God the Son, and God the Holy Spirit has been an unfolding mystery, unfurling down through the corridors of history. This doesn't mean the ineffable mystery of the Trinity is comparable to the historical mystery of the *who* and the *where* of these "other people." But in the case of God's choice of when to reveal His plans for certain individuals, there does seem to be a certain logic as to why God sometimes chooses to hide His choice, as He clearly did with these various migrations to which I'm referring.

A Bodyguard of Lies

IN MANY ways, when we analyze the secret, private nature of the scattering of lost Israel, spoken of by Micah and Hosea, we're actually seeing the secret, private nature of God, in terms of the subterfuge any student of military history encounters. In this instance, though, we're dealing with a case study not in human warfare but in nothing less than the ages-long tug of war between God and Satan for the soul of humanity. As such, I want to emphasize that just as certain tactics in human warfare are required for one side to win that war, the same applies in spiritual warfare. It's even appropriate in this regard to quote Winston Churchill, who said, "In war, truth is so precious she must be surrounded by a bodyguard of lies."

As for the war of the ages between God and Satan, ask yourself: Has God withheld information at any point in history in order to defeat the devil in his attack on humanity? Of course I can't help but think He has. Again, the curse of knowledge sometimes has us forgetting that the devil isn't omniscient; we forget that he doesn't know everything about God's plan until He unfolds it, chapter by chapter.

As such, the devil doesn't understand the Incarnation, or the meaning of prophecy, or what the Holy Spirit would accomplish with the death and resurrection of Christ. If anything, Satan's even more surprised by what Christ accomplished through His life, death, and resurrection than we are because, unlike us, he's not bound by time and space. He's been along for the ride during every phase of God's expanding Empire. So, if the devil isn't smart enough to understand what God is up to, with His game of spiritual cat and mouse, then why can't we as Christians admit we face the same dilemma?

Which leads me finally to the jumping-off point to one of the most important private migrations found in the canonical record. It's important because if we can establish that it really is there in *The Old Testament*, then no one can maintain the same old argument that there's no canonical evidence to confirm the whereabouts of these "other people" in "another place."

Just as importantly, we'll also better understand why God chose to fly these migrations "under the radar" with minimal fanfare. He did so to ensure the devil would be so caught off guard by these end-run maneuvers he'd never be able to recover his former dominance over the hearts and minds of humanity.

Having examined the migrations that occurred in the days of Noah, Abraham, Jacob, Joseph, and both kingdoms of Israel and Judah, let's turn next to another pivotal migration of critical importance. In doing so, I hope to pinpoint further the location and identity of those "other people," which Moses, Nathan, Daniel, and Jesus had in mind. However, while all these other migrations involved a great mass of people on the move, this one involved a mere handful of players. There were the daughters of a doomed king of Judah, who also happened to be the grandnieces of a famed Hebrew prophet who led the group, along with the prophet's scribe and a minor contingency, which comprised the prophet's entourage of fellow wanderers and outcasts.

The Judahite king's name was Zedekiah, the prophet's scribe's name was Baruch, the king's daughters' names were Tea Tephi and Tea Scota, and the Hebrew prophet's name was Jeremiah.

Chapter Sixteen

JEREMIAH AND HIS MISSION

*The words of the Lord are pure words, as
silver tried in a furnace of Earth, purified
seven times. You will keep them, oh Lord. You
preserve them from this generation forever.
(Psalm 12:6-7)*

Crossroads of History

THE YEAR was 583 B.C. Just three years earlier the city of Jerusalem had been sacked by Nebuchadnezzar of Babylon, and King Zedekiah was forced to watch as all his sons were slain before his eyes. Then those same eyes were put out, and they would see no more. So ended the line of the kings of Judah, according to traditional biblical history; so ended the royal line of David, say those biblical traditionalists who apparently have decided to ignore the testimony of numerous sources in Scripture, such as *Second Samuel* and the *Psalms*.

So if the traditional view of biblical history tells us one thing, then what are we to do with verses that clearly tell us something altogether different? First, Nathan, the prophet, said to King David, concerning God's intention:

He'll build a house for My name, and I'll establish the throne of his kingdom forever. I'll be his Father, and he'll be My son… But My loving devotion will never be removed from him as I removed it from Saul, whom I moved out of your way. Your house and kingdom will endure forever before Me, and your throne will be established forever.[153]

The psalmist then confirmed this when he had God saying:

I won't violate My covenant or alter what My lips have uttered. Once and for all, I've sworn by My holiness; I won't lie to David. His line will continue forever and his throne endure before Me like the Sun; it will be established forever like the Moon, the faithful witness in the sky.[154]

So if there's any truth to what Nathan and the psalmist said, then why doesn't our traditional view of biblical history confirm the existence of this perpetual royal dynasty of David? Of course, to anyone following the storyline presented here, the answer to this riddle might already seem obvious. The answer falls in the category of those times when God has chosen to act inconspicuously in order to blindside the devil who is trying to thwart God's choice of who will fulfill the commission of taking His truth to the whole world.

In this case, we find that a critical aspect of God's faithfulness toward an onlooking world has been aborted with the apparent end of David's royal line, which in turn has created a major blind spot in the eyes of Bible-believers the world over. In response to this assumed failure on God's part to protect and preserve this promised Davidic line, two views have developed. On one hand, believers have no choice but to spiritualize this promise of God and so make Jesus the fulfillment of this promise, which still evades the unanswered question of how the enormous gap between Zedekiah and Jesus confirms God's faithfulness. And on the other hand, unbelievers have a field day with this historical *faux pas* in their attempt to undermine a genuine faith in God's control over history, thereby insisting that if David's royal line ceased with the death of Zedekiah, then clearly God's word is worthless.

---

153   *Second Samuel 7:13-16*

154   *Psalm 89:34-37*

This is, of course, why it's so important to remind ourselves, as believers in God's faithfulness, that God's ways aren't our ways, and just because we presume that God only acts how we expect Him to act, He often acts quite differently. So just as Elijah was pleasantly surprised that God had a much better way of rescuing him in his hour of need, by way of God's still, small voice, we too should never fail to realize that God's preferred method of salvation is always that which flies "under the radar."

Fortunately, for us, we have Jeremiah and his mission to verify this. Let's take some time, then, to investigate Jeremiah's story in the context of what I'm calling the interplay between God's way of doing things conspicuously and inconspicuously, publicly and privately. That's because when it comes to this chapter in the biblical narrative, Jeremiah just happens to play out his role at perhaps one of the most critical crossroads of history. Why do I say that? I do so because when it comes to analyzing the various histories we find in *The Bible*, so many of them are prone to being questioned because of their remoteness in time in relation to our present day. In short, the further along our present moves forward into the future, the more distant do the ancient tales of Scripture recede backward into the past. As a result, it's very easy for critics to contest the validity of these stories and for believers to question whether they can still be trusted because they happened so long ago.

Another way of looking at this problem is to remind ourselves of the uniqueness of American history. Compared to the origins of other countries in this world, ours is so young that while past events are always subject to error and exaggeration, they're still much less susceptible to error and exaggeration than when we examine the origins of, say, England, France, or Germany.

Preserving His Word for All Generations

OF COURSE, the most important thing to remember when we read *The Bible* is that, while it contains a written record of our distant past, there's one thing about it that we can count on, as opposed to the written records of any other nation in world history. And that is, the veracity of the scriptural record is such that it's entirely dependent upon the integrity of God Himself. In other words, while other historical records claim to report the origins of the nations, *The Bible* is uniquely said to be a *protected* record of national origins.

Naturally, this point is always open for debate, as is everything else about the meaning and message of Scripture; but it's still something to consider when debating the truthfulness of *The Bible*. Said the psalmist: "Forever, oh Lord, Your word is settled in Heaven."[155] And again:

> The words of the Lord are pure words, as silver tried in a furnace of Earth, purified seven times. You will keep them, oh Lord. You preserve them from this generation forever.[156]

If anything, then, when it comes to the historical record in Scripture, although translation issues can water down the potential meaning of certain passages, which then requires further analyses to clarify, we can still be certain the God of *The Bible* is fully committed to preserving His word for all generations.

I mention all this now because it's so easy to forget that when we talk about various periods of history, people naturally lean toward either skepticism or belief because of their various perspectives about the nature of historical evidence. That is to say, some people have no problem with the historicity of *The New Testament* but have a hard time accepting anything in *The Old Testament*. When asked why this is the case, one might say that it's because events described in *The New Testament* are far more credible than those in *The Old Testament*. For them, it's easier to verify the events surrounding Peter and Paul's ministry to the Romans than it is to confirm Moses and Joshua's role in leading the Children of Israel to the Promised Land. Then there are those for which certain events described in *The Old Testament* are valid, while others are not. For example, stories of Abraham, Isaac, and Jacob are believed with no problem, yet they remain skeptical about stories of Enoch, Seth, or Adam.

Naturally, the dividing line is drawn in reference to a differ-

---

155   *Psalm 119:89*

156   *Ibid. 12:6-7*

ence in historical time. According to this way of thinking, the further back in time that describe stories of biblical figures, the more doubtful they become and so are deemed too ancient to be considered valid representations of the past.

Outcasts and Wanderers

WITH THAT in mind, we embark upon the next leg of our journey, in connecting Israel of old, the Kingdom of Stone, and America today, in which we turn to the story of Jeremiah and his wards: the two royal daughters of King Zedekiah. What I'm most concerned about here is that while stories of Noah, Abraham, and Jesus have so far provided the majority of our clues in pursuit of this connection, most Christians have no problem accepting them because they're stories firmly rooted in the biblical tradition. No doubt, some of the verses to which I've pointed may seem foreign because mainstream Christianity rarely talks about them. However, because they're clearly there to read in the scriptural record, they can't be discounted or disbelieved on the grounds that they're unscriptural.

Unfortunately, the same can't be said when we delve into the unusual story of Jeremiah and his wards. That's because, in this instance, we'll be dealing with the all-too-human tendency to dismiss historical evidence because it's outside of traditionally accepted periods of time that are deemed trustworthy by most historians. Such events that we'll be turning to next are more often than not reduced to the status of legend or myth, and therefore are subject to the same skepticism leveled by critics of *The Bible*.

That's why it's also important to remember that other aspect of our investigation that I previously mentioned, which is that before we even begin to search out matters of biblical import, we first need to establish that Jesus warranted such investigations. No doubt if the prophets of old, like Moses and Nathan, spoke of that "other people" being transplanted to that "other place," that by itself could be considered sufficient cause to look for them. But when Jesus Himself spoke of the kingdom being relocated to another land, where they'd finally fulfill God's purposes, then that, in my view, seals the deal. Then that is enough to look for the evidence—historical, geographical, philological, archeological, or otherwise.

Then, upon finding this evidence in sufficient amounts, I'm led to ask the next logical question: If this evidence doesn't confirm that this other people and other place are the ones that God's prophets spoke of, then *who* or *where* do you suggest we look instead?

That's because, the bottom line is: You can't have it both ways. God's word is clear on the existence of these people and that place, so you can't just close your eyes and pretend a people as numerous as the dust of the Earth or the sand of the sea doesn't exist. And if you claim that God's word is trustworthy, then history must confirm the location of a place that's capable of containing these dust-like people; and it must confirm the existence of the royal descendants of that Davidic line that accompany sand-like people who comprise a multitude of nations.

But fear not, history does reveal where those people are and where that royal line went, and we have Jeremiah and his band of outcasts and wanderers to help us find out where that place is. Just as importantly, we can thank two other groups of outcasts and wanderers who will aid us in our quest to find that place. First, we must acknowledge the role of those exiled "lost sheep of the House of Israel," whom we learned about in a previous chapter, and whom we'll learn more about in subsequent chapters. Second, we must acknowledge those who comprised the first wave of Israelite migrants, the sons and daughters of Zarah, the twin brother of Pharez and royal son of Judah. Because as we'll discover in the chapters that follow, these Zarahites were actually the original group of migrants, in this ages-long story, who fled Egypt before the rest of the family fell into bondage after Joseph's death, and before Moses led the more familiar group of Israelites out from the land of the pharaohs.

In point of fact, I'm talking about a three-pronged migration of the Children of Israel, all three aspects of which were divinely designed to "fly under the radar" to blindside Satan's endless quest to derail God's plan to manifest His Kingdom on Earth. In doing so, we'll show how these migrations fulfill God's promise to bless all nations through Abraham and his descendants;

they'll fulfill Daniel's vision of the Stone Kingdom destroying the corrupt kingdoms of this world and then overspreading the entire planet; and finally, in tying all this together in historical terms, we'll be telling the ultimate tale that is the promise of America, technology, and the New Earth.

THIS CONCLUDES *On Earth as It is On Heaven, Book One.* To read further, please refer to the next book in this series, entitled *On Earth as It is On Heaven, Book Two.* Or, if you prefer, you may read the entire work, which contains all three books in a single volume, by referring to *On Earth as It is On Heaven: The Promise of America, Technology, and the New Earth.* To get this publication, or an eBook version of this text, go to *The Lost Stories Channel* at loststorieschannel.com, or Amazon Books.

Additionally, for those of you who are so inclined, please post a positive review on Amazon so that others might become aware of its valuable contents. Because this book was not published by a conglomerate-style publishing house, we rely more heavily on word-of-mouth to advertise its importance to others who, like yourself, are searching for books like this. Thank you for your support.

ABOUT THE AUTHOR

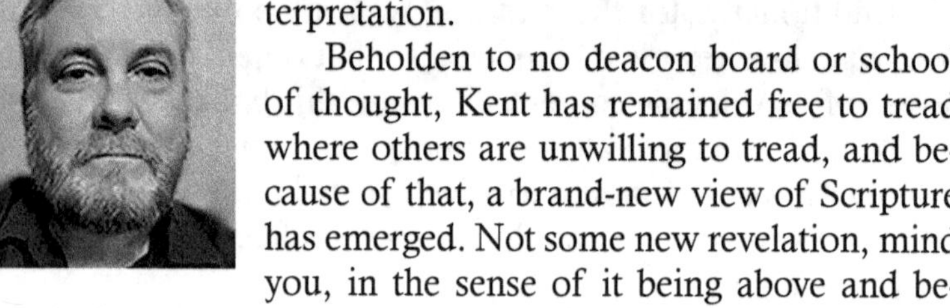

FOR MORE than forty years, W. Kent Smith has immersed himself in the teachings of the greatest biblical scholars of the ages—William Barclay, C.S. Lewis, W. Gene Scott, *et al*. More importantly during that time, he has immersed himself in *The Bible* itself. Add to that, Kent's unique perspective on history, humanity, and life, and the result is a one-of-a-kind take on biblical history and theology. What that means to you as a fellow truth seeker is a message unhindered by many outmoded traditions of biblical interpretation.

Beholden to no deacon board or school of thought, Kent has remained free to tread where others are unwilling to tread, and because of that, a brand-new view of Scripture has emerged. Not some new revelation, mind you, in the sense of it being above and beyond *The Bible* itself. What we are talking about is a fresh understanding of what Scripture has been saying all along, one that's been hidden in plain sight, waiting for someone to connect the dots, to reveal a picture that's been lying dormant until now.

Kent lives in West Covina, California, an eastern suburb of Los Angeles. He can be contacted at wkent@loststorieschannel.com, or lodestarcinema@msn.com.